Love Stroke

Love Stroke

Stroke Recovery and One Young Couple's Journey

Kelly and Brad Marsh

LOVE STROKE
STROKE RECOVERY AND ONE YOUNG COUPLE'S JOURNEY

iUniverse books may be ordered through booksellers or by contacting:

iUniverse
1663 Liberty Drive
Bloomington, IN 47403
www.iuniverse.com
1-800-Authors (1-800-288-4677)

ISBN: 978-1-5320-0287-8 (sc)
ISBN: 978-1-5320-0286-1 (e)

Library of Congress Control Number: 2016914253

Print information available on the last page.

iUniverse rev. date: 10/21/2016

This book is dedicated to my loving husband, family, friends, and all the amazing surgeons, doctors, nurses, and therapists that helped be along the way. I cannot thank you enough!

CONTENTS

FOREWORD

I am a neurologist and a stroke specialist. I can honestly tell the reader that being a doctor can be difficult for many reasons (not the least of which is trying to survive each day of work within the chaos that is our current health care system), but it is an incredibly rewarding job. Why? Every day we try to help our patients deal with medical problems and improve their function and quality of life. Seeing how diseases, such as stroke, affect our patients makes us deeply grateful for health in both ourselves and our loved ones, and seeing how families pull together in times of crisis is inspiring and makes us appreciate our own relationships with family and friends. In the aftermath of the devastating attacks on September 11, 2001, many people struggled to find meaning in their everyday jobs. I can honestly say that I had no such problem—I find great meaning in my job every day, as I am honored to work with stroke patients and their caregivers.

Stroke is a uniquely difficult disease that is currently the number-five cause of death and one of the leading causes of disability among adults in the United States. Symptoms come on suddenly, and within minutes, a young, healthy woman, such as Kelly, the heroine of this book, can have a significant injury to her brain. Once the brain is injured, the affected area dies and cannot heal or regrow. The functions that the affected part of the brain served are immediately lost, and the recovery process is managed by neuroplasticity, which is the ability of the surviving brain to take over the functions that were lost. This process has two stages. The first stage, which this book notes as taking approximately six months, is the spontaneous phase. During this time, recovery will happen even if the patient does no therapy; however, doing therapy during this phase is generally thought to facilitate recovery. Most improvements in function occur in the first days to weeks, and by six months, progress slows, as the spontaneous phase has largely ended. Thereafter, the recovery process can continue, but the process is much more difficult. We used to say that function plateaus and will not get better after six to twelve months, but this is simply not true. However, recovery after the spontaneous phase is slow, and other problems, such as spasticity, joint contractures, or falls, can offset progress.

Stroke can change someone's life in an instant. The poststroke recovery process is a long, hard road—it is truly a marathon and not a sprint—and stroke recovery is a team sport, as the stroke survivor needs help.

This book, written by a young stroke survivor and her husband/caregiver (the roles are not separate), is filled with some great advice for stroke survivors and their loved ones. I was fascinated to read it, because while I had read other such books, I had never yet read one written by a patient of mine. Despite having taken a full history of Kelly's stroke and seen her in clinic on many occasions, I did not know many parts of her story and certainly did not know her inner thoughts and emotions. I was fascinated to hear the details from both perspectives, especially from Kelly in her own words. Her aphasia has recovered greatly, but her spoken language during clinic visits has not been as rich as this writing. It should be noted that different functions improve at different rates—movement and strength are easiest, and we know more about how to help these functions recover. Other functions, such as language, improve more slowly and less completely. We are not sure that vision or sensation can meaningfully improve, and cognitive function improves slowly, if at all. There is little research available about these latter functions.

My admission above shows how difficult the practice of medicine is. It is a challenge to really know someone when only short visits occur and when the focus of those visits is all business, targeted to specific issues that must be addressed. Furthermore, there is much that we truly just don't know yet, especially when dealing with an organ as complex as the brain. Despite ongoing research, there are many questions that your providers simply do not know the answers to. This is an inconvenient truth, but it must be said.

In this book, Kelly and Brad, at times, are critical of the health care system. The criticisms are fair and highlight a challenge of stroke recovery—our system involves many types of providers (multiple different kinds of doctors, therapists, etc.) and is often lacking in overarching care management. Despite detailed medical records, communication between providers is difficult, at least in part because there is too much to read and we are all busy, trying to work quickly and efficiently. Insurance companies can be difficult to deal with, to say the least, for health care providers and for patients and loved ones. I hope we will continue to improve our process of care locally and across the United States and world to help stroke survivors recover more fully and with less stress. In the meanwhile, networking with other survivors and utilizing hints like the ones in this book are necessary and useful.

I have focused my practice and research on stroke outcomes and recovery because I have been inspired by watching stroke survivors and their caregivers work to improve their postinjury function and quality of life. Events like the yearly 1K Steps for Stroke, mentioned in the book, during which we witness a stroke survivor walk a thousand kilometers for the first time since his or her stroke, are inspiring beyond words. I marvel that humans have climbed Mount Everest but am no less impressed that stroke survivors find the strength, courage, and fortitude to regain lost function and accomplish their own Everest-like tasks. I am more impressed by Kelly making a lasagna with one good arm than a healthy athlete running a marathon.

The authors, Kelly and Brad, are wonderful people to know, and as demonstrated in the book, they are clearly very much in love. It has been my privilege to be involved with their efforts toward Kelly's recovery and to get to know them better via reading this book.

As a parting thought, I have often thought that maybe heaven for a stroke doctor will include the ability to know all of his or her patients as they were before the stroke—it is impossible for me not to wonder at times what it would have been like to meet Kelly and my other patients before their stroke. But as Kelly and Brad point out, it is sometimes through unwanted events, such as a stroke, that people evolve in a positive fashion. While unwanted, the stroke has changed Kelly and Brad in some ways for the better, both as individuals and as a married couple. This is an important lesson for all readers of this book: out of difficulty and hardship, we can more truly experience love and fulfillment. So while I can't help but be curious about what my stroke patients were like pre-stroke, I wouldn't trade my relationships with the people they are now for anything.

If you are a stroke survivor, I wish you good luck on your journey to recovery. You must define your own sweet spot for quality of life, and I urge you to stay determined until you get there. If you are a caregiver, I hope you will find joy and love in helping your stroke survivor. And I hope that your medical team can help you both along this journey.

Best wishes,

Brett M. Kissela, MD, MS
Albert Barnes Voorheis professor and chair
Department of Neurology and Rehabilitation Medicine
University of Cincinnati

PREFACE

Every year in the United States, stroke affects nearly eight hundred thousand people* and millions of caregivers. Having a stroke completely changes your life, and these changes can make caregivers or survivors feel as if they are alone. Despite how it might feel, we would like to say that you are not alone, and we hope our book helps in some way during a difficult time for you and your loved one.

Love Stroke was inspired by our experiences and our wish that there were more books on the market to help people understand what is happening and make the best decisions possible during this challenging time of unknowns and important life and relationship decisions. We also wish we would have known more about stroke and its early and later stage signs, which might have prevented what happened to us. Like many other younger people in the prime of our lives and careers, we never would have thought that some of the early signs could be those of something serious, much less a stroke, which we both thought was some form of a heart attack.

Our story is intended to be both practical and inspirational for all traumatic brain injury survivors and caregivers, particularly younger survivors and caregivers as they shape their own destinies in recovery. We believe it is the only book of its kind—one that shares the firsthand chronological views of both the survivor and the primary caregiver (Kelly

* "Stroke Facts," Centers for Disease Control and Prevention, accessed February 2016, http://www.cdc.gov/stroke/facts.htm.

and Brad), including our life before, the day everything changed, and the first two years of recovery.

Love Stroke is a carefully chosen title meant to represent the conflicting, frightening, and enlightening experiences and feelings we went through as a result of a traumatic brain injury, which, in our case, was a near-fatal hemorrhagic stroke.

We will share personal trial-and-error insights from our journey and challenge some conventional medical wisdom about what is possible. We will offer advice to friends and family on the best way to support their loved ones and each other, and we will include some of the resources we found useful and lessons we learned along the way that we wish someone had shared with us. The narrative is supported by "If We Only Knew" lessons at the end of most chapters, which give helpful tips for those who are in need of quick ideas. We've also included a section of lessons learned, suggested reading, website recommendations, and a START assessment example in the appendices.

Love Stroke will also help educate the majority of readers who have not yet been impacted by stroke but want to understand more about it and how to proactively manage risk for themselves and loved ones who might be showing signs or have health practices that increase risk.

Our story doesn't end with this book. We will be using some of the proceeds from *Love Stroke* to start our new foundation, A Stroke Forward (ASF). The foundation will focus on providing young caregivers and survivors with critical resources needed to make the most of their recovery. There are currently insurance limitations and minimal resources available for survivors when they need them most (in the first twelve months), and ASF plans to focus on helping this growing population in the prime of their personal and professional lives regain as much of their independence and ability as possible.

While there are still daily challenges and not all the things we used to do are possible, we truly believe our stroke made us stronger as individuals and as a couple. We hope our story helps people better navigate all the challenges life can bring and provides an example of what is possible with hard work, trust, and commitment.

Remember as you read that everything could change tomorrow.

CHAPTER 1

The Day Everything Changed

Kelly

In August 2009, my husband, Brad, and I took an early anniversary trip: a long weekend to New Orleans. Since our wedding in September 2005, both of our careers had picked up pace and intensity. Brad was traveling a lot, often internationally, and my position as chief marketing officer at a local Catholic college had me working long hours. Sometimes I felt as if the only chance I got to slow down and stop thinking about work, family, and other stress was at daily Mass.

Even off the clock, we played hard: Brad was an avid golfer, we had many opportunities to travel, we held season tickets to Xavier University men's basketball and were frequently in the stands at Cincinnati Bengals and Reds games, and we spent much of each summer with my family at their riverside camp in Warsaw, Kentucky.

By the time summer wound down in 2009, we agreed we needed a chance to relax, just the two of us. New Orleans seemed like the perfect place to unwind and reconnect.

I had had a steady, dull headache on the right side of my head for about a week before the trip. Not being prone to headaches as a rule, I attributed it to my stress about work and the hectic schedule I had been keeping. Now that the new professors were on board and the students had returned to campus, I had a few days of relative calm, so I could take some time off to recharge my batteries.

We stayed at the newly remodeled Roosevelt Hotel and did our version of a relaxing vacation—which, of course, meant a nearly nonstop schedule. We saw all the local architectural and historical sights, visited several museums, and enjoyed the famous New Orleans food and jazz. We even went on a swamp-boat tour that boasted the chance to see alligators to round out our Big Easy experience.

Though I had a good time, my head continued to ache all weekend. As we rode to the airport to return to Cincinnati, I felt a little nauseated. It wasn't unusual for me to have some motion sickness in a car, so I didn't think much of it at that moment.

Brad and I had been talking about our fantasy football draft, which was scheduled for that afternoon at three o'clock. We had even taken an earlier flight home so we'd be sure not to miss the draft. We passed the time in flight looking at my teams, discussing the players, and deciding whom to draft in which round. It was probably the most we'd slowed down and relaxed on the whole trip.

We landed at about one thirty, right on time, and walked to the baggage claim together. Once we got our bags, Brad stepped into the bathroom to freshen up.

The minute he walked away, I went from feeling fine to not fine at all. I could feel my face flushing and thought, *I'm going to vomit. I need air!* I desperately wanted to get out of the airport immediately, forgetting that it was August 30 and that the air outside was likely even more stifling. I didn't understand it; I just knew I needed to get outside.

I exited through the automatic doors, breathing consciously. *In. Out. In. Out.* Still, I was feeling worse by the second. I did not just feel ill; I felt strange, as if I were outside my body. The sensation made me want to laugh out loud, only I found that something was wrong with my lips.

Shake it off, Kel. Focus. Relax, I told myself. *Go back inside and find Brad.* But I couldn't move. My body wouldn't let me.

Food. Need to eat something. I get light-headed when my blood sugar is low, so I was in the habit of carrying a snack. That day, I had an apple with me, and I managed to get it out of my bag and bring it to my mouth.

I took a bite and then watched as the apple rolled out of my hand seemingly in slow motion, bounced twice, and came to a stop a few feet away on the concrete.

What the hell? I thought. I saw a hand reach for the apple. *Wait—is that my hand? Why can't I feel it?*

Something was really wrong, and I couldn't ignore or explain it. My heart raced in my chest. Was that panic or something else? People moved past me in a blur, two amorphous blobs where it seemed only one person should be. Sounds came to me muffled, as though I were underwater.

Am I in a time warp? My mind grasped blindly for explanations.

Dazed, I leaned against the wall and hit the speed dial for Brad on my cell phone. I received no answer. I then tried to text him. "Please help," I wanted to write, but I found that I couldn't press the buttons on my BlackBerry. In fact, my right hand didn't seem to be working at all, and my eyes couldn't focus.

Maybe this is what it feels like to be on LSD.

I looked around at the people passing by. I tried to call out, "Somebody, help me!" but no sound came out. My body was shutting down one function at a time. My legs buckled, my arms hung limply at my sides, and my lips and tongue felt paralyzed.

I felt my breathing speed up and become shallow. I was hyperventilating.

I'm suffocating. Somebody, help me!

Finally, I saw Brad coming out the doors with his cell phone in hand, scanning the area for me.

"Kelly! What's wrong? What is it?" He was running now, and he reached me in seconds.

I moved my lips. Or maybe I wasn't moving my lips. I couldn't tell anymore.

He looks worried. Why is he so worried? What's happening?

I collapsed into him and blacked out. My next thought was *Is this an ambulance? I've never been on the inside of an ambulance before. White—everything is white. I'm dreaming. This is just a crazy, vivid dream.*

Faces hovered over me, calling my name.

If it's only a dream, then why am I so scared?

I lost consciousness again.

Brad

"I'm going to clean up and change into my shorts," I told Kelly after we picked up our bags.

While I was in the bathroom, my phone rang, but I couldn't get to it right away. When I did, I noticed that I had missed a call from Kelly.

Weird, I thought. *Why would she be calling me?*

Then I saw that I had two text messages from her. The first read, "hep mp," and the next text was a jumble of letters that didn't make sense.

What the hell? I wondered.

I rushed out of the bathroom but didn't see Kelly where I'd left her at the baggage carousel. I stepped outside and found her leaning with her back against the glass wall.

There was an apple on the ground with one bite out of it, and her phone was lying beside it on the pavement.

"Help me. Help me," she mumbled.

"What's wrong, Kelly? What's wrong?" I could hear my voice rising a little in panic.

"I don't know." Her speech was slurred, barely intelligible. "I can't feel my face and even my tongue."

"Do you want me to get help?"

"I don't know," she said, just looking at me, petrified.

Time seemed to slow as I stood with her, trying to figure out what to do. It felt like forever, though probably only two or three minutes passed. In those few minutes, she could no longer talk or hold herself up.

As I held her up against the window glass, my panic grew. One of the airport's ground transportation drivers waiting by the curb saw me struggling and said, "Hey, do you need help? Do you need me to call an ambulance?"

"I don't know. I don't know what's going on. She—yeah, but I can't leave her, so yeah, if you can call somebody …" My voice trailed off as I turned back to Kelly. "It's going to be okay," I told her, not knowing if that was true.

Someone else came to help me hold her up, and another Good Samaritan rolled out an airport wheelchair. By the time the EMTs showed up, she was fading in and out of consciousness. They tried to assess her status, but she couldn't talk to them clearly, so they both helped me get her into the wheelchair.

Once she was seated, the EMTs started going through their checklist of questions: "What were you doing when this started? Can you describe what kind of pain you're in? Where is the pain? How severe is it?"

She was attempting to respond, but even her vague yes, no, or "I don't know" replies were slurred, and alarmingly, foam was forming on her mouth. She passed out, at which point they put her on a stretcher and rolled her into the ambulance as I stood helplessly on the pavement.

"We're getting a response now," one paramedic said a moment later. "That's a good sign."

"Well, should we go to the emergency room?" I was still in disbelief that this could be happening to Kelly. "She was fine just a few minutes ago."

"Absolutely we're going to the emergency room," he said. "For sure, to the closest hospital. You can follow us."

As I hurried toward my car in the short-term parking lot, I called Kelly's sister-in-law Mindy.

"I don't know what's going on, so don't panic until I know more. But Kelly had something happen to her. She lost consciousness, so we're going to the nearest hospital to have her checked out. I'll let you know when I find out more."

While driving from the airport to the hospital, I thought about a friend of ours who had had a TIA (transient ischemic attack—a kind of ministroke), but I didn't know what that really meant. I just knew that she had some issues and now took an aspirin.

Maybe it's something like that. Maybe it's not that serious.

How could it be something serious? Kelly was young, fit, and healthy. I kept telling myself that anybody could pass out or experience numbness for lots of different reasons.

I actually beat the EMTs to the hospital, and I spent those precious minutes filling out paperwork at the front desk of the emergency room.

By the time they let me back to see Kelly, she was having significant tremors. Her legs bounced up and down, her mouth and face were twitching uncontrollably, and her eyes just stared into space. Her eyes were open, but she wasn't responding, just looking out.

The look in her eyes is impossible to describe. Terror, despair, numbness, unconsciousness—it's hard to say, but I had never seen anything like it.

The doctor on call had already run an MRI and said they needed to get her to a neurologist ASAP. There wasn't a neurologist available at this hospital, so she needed to go to one of two other facilities in the area that had neurological staff on Sundays, whichever was first available. Through my haze of shock, I heard the word *surgery*.

"Surgery?" I repeated.

"We can't really get into details here. You need to go with her to the next hospital, and they'll take care of you over there."

That was when I knew it was bad. It had only been an hour since we'd landed in Cincinnati, but it seemed as though days had passed.

Operating on autopilot, I beat Kelly's arrival to the next place as well, which meant I had a moment to call her family. "We're not going to be there for the fantasy football draft," I said. "I'm going into the second hospital right now. This is something more serious than I originally thought, and I hope to know more soon. Can someone come down here?"

I couldn't ignore the possibility that the situation might require a decision for which I would want support.

At about three thirty, I went back to talk to the neurosurgeon. Kelly lay quietly on the bed, sedated to control the seizures.

The surgeon was matter-of-fact with me. "Kelly's got about a two-inch-diameter hemorrhage right here," he said, pointing it out to me on the MRI. "She's continuing to bleed, and that's what's causing the issues with her feeling and movements."

He didn't call it a stroke but said it was a hemorrhage, which I knew meant bleeding, but I didn't truly understand what he was describing. This didn't seem important at the time, but anyone who knew what a stroke was would have realized what had happened. I only mention it because for a couple of days, I couldn't explain to friends and family what had happened. They asked if it was a stroke, and I said no because the doctor had said there was bleeding and had not used the word *stroke*.

He explained that a rupture had likely occurred in one of Kelly's blood vessels, resulting in blood engulfing brain tissue and spreading quickly. In such a situation, the blood engulfs the brain cells and stops oxygen from getting to them as it should. With their oxygen supply cut off, the brain cells cannot function correctly and eventually die. The result of the suffocating cells is loss of control and function of the parts of the body controlled by that section of the brain.

"We've got a couple of options. We can let it go and hope it stops. There's going to be damage at this stage, probably significant—it's hard to tell."

I sat there, stunned, trying to absorb this information.

"So you know, we can do nothing. She won't be the way she was. But if we do nothing, I'd say that gives her a fifty-fifty shot," he said. "Or we can operate right away; we can remove the hematoma, drain the blood, and try to stop it. Someone her age should regain some of her faculties and capabilities, but we won't know until it's done and she's recovered."

"Wait," I said. "Go back. A fifty-fifty shot at what?"

"Surviving," he said. "Making it."

"So let me get this straight," I said, holding back my tears and shock as the weight of his words started to sink in. "If we don't operate, she's got a fifty-fifty shot, and if she makes it, we don't know what kind of state her brain will be in? And if we operate, she's got a real good chance of making it through at her age, and the damage will be limited to whatever brain cells are dead now?"

"Yes."

"Well, what does that mean? What kind of damage are we talking about?"

"We won't know until it's done and she's recovered. The blood that has leaked is toxic to her brain cells wherever it makes contact, so it can continue to cause damage until it stops on its own, which it may not. Or until we stop it."

Up until that afternoon, the only decisions I'd expected to make that day were about my fantasy football draft. I was completely unprepared for something like this. They hadn't covered this in the Pre-Cana classes.

Eventually, I said, "That seems like an obvious choice to me."

Doctors have opinions, but they are trained to present your choices as factually and objectively as possible and to avoid pressuring family into decisions. So I phrased my next question in such a way as to at least get him off the fence and concur that probably the best move was to have the surgery.

"So what's our timeline? How quickly … Do you need to know right now?"

"Well, time is pretty critical right now. If we're going to go, we need to go. We need to operate sooner rather than later, because every minute counts. But you've got twenty to thirty minutes to decide."

I said, "Doctor, her family is very close. I am her husband, but I don't know that her family would want me to make that decision without consulting them. I'd like to confer with Kelly's parents and her brothers and sisters; hopefully they are here right now. Could you relay to them what you just told me? I don't know that I can adequately articulate it."

At the time, taking twenty to thirty minutes to consult with Kelly's family made sense to me. I believed that Kelly would have wanted me to involve them in the decision. I didn't understand that literally every minute during a bleed means more damaged brain cells. If I had understood the signs of stroke and what was really happening, I would have done things differently. I for sure would have requested the EMTs take her to a hospital with neurosurgery capabilities in case she needed them, rather than making two stops. I would have pushed for a faster diagnosis, though all the tests take time. But how could I have known? I couldn't have unless I had been through it. Still, I regret losing those precious minutes for her.

We walked out to the waiting room and found Kelly's family waiting. The doctor described our options, and they looked to me for an opinion.

I said, "I think we should have surgery." They agreed absolutely.

So within three hours of landing at the airport, Kelly was heading into brain surgery.

I stood with Kelly's family and watched through my tears as the attendants wheeled her into the operating room. Word had traveled fast, and soon the group expanded to include aunts and uncles, the remaining brothers and sisters, and my parents. We waited, pacing, and finally gathered in the hallway.

Holding hands, we prayed the Lord's Prayer.

Waiting for Answers

In the back of my mind, I thought about how our day had begun—leaving New Orleans and heading home for the fantasy football draft after some needed time together on vacation. I thought about our life together, our plans, and our future, and I wondered what was in store for us.

I couldn't help but remember the last time we'd gone on vacation and wound up in a hospital. It was four years prior in Aruba, on our honeymoon, which was a gift from my parents.

We enjoyed two days there in the tropics before we were sidelined, because Kelly promptly got an eye infection. The whole side of her face was swollen, and she was miserable.

We were lucky to find an eye doctor near the hotel, and when we left his office, Kelly had a huge eye patch that went all the way around her head. I could tell she felt our honeymoon was ruined. "I can't even have fun. I can't be outside. I can't go to dinner. I can't do anything!" I heard her tell her mom over the phone.

The next day, Kelly went out wearing sunglasses to hide the eye patch. It wasn't ideal, but she was a trooper and was determined to have a good time in less-than-ideal conditions. A couple of times, she drew an eye on the outside of the eye patch just to be funny.

Now I found myself in a waiting room again, and I wondered if this would ever be a story we could look back on with laughter or even relief. I couldn't even think about making the best of it yet, not when there were still so many questions.

One thing was certain: everything was different. Everything had changed.

If We Only Knew: Warning Signs and Actions

- An easy acronym to remember for stroke warning signs is FAST, which stands for face, arms, speech, and time.

  F: Ask the person to smile. Does one side of the face droop?

  A: Observe the person's arms. Arm weakness or the inability to hold both arms up is another sign of stroke.

S: Listen for slurred or strange speech and other speech difficulties.

T: If you notice these symptoms, it's time to call 911. (Please also visit the National Stroke Association's website, which appears on the list of website resources at the end of the book, to learn more.)

- If you suspect a stroke or see evidence of any of the above symptoms, know that time is critical. Get the person to the hospital as soon as possible and, if an option, a hospital with a neurology unit.

- If you are in a public place, ask for help quickly, as you will soon need assistance.

- If surgery is recommended, move fast. The thirty minutes I took to confirm with Kelly's family to have surgery might have cost her ability. Maybe not, but nothing is more critical than time, because the damage continues until the cause of the stroke is fixed.

CHAPTER 2

Now What?

Brad

"She made it," the surgeon said. "The surgery was successful."

Relief washed over me, and Kelly's parents embraced silently. We could all finally exhale.

I had been thinking only about Kelly's survival for the past two hours. We were through the surgery now, but what did that mean? *Now what?*

"She presented with a two-inch bleed in the left hemisphere of the brain that was relieved by craniotomy, which means we removed a portion of her skullcap," the surgeon explained. "We didn't find an aneurysm or anything else suspicious. It's possible it washed out when we irrigated the excess blood in her brain; perhaps we missed it. Regardless, we can't tell what caused the bleed. A blood vessel or multiple blood vessels burst, but we don't know why."

Despite the uncertainties, I knew what I needed to know for that moment: she was alive.

Kelly's family and I walked together back to her room. She was sleeping, lying perfectly still in the bed, with bandages covering her head and a mask on her face. Machines whirred and beeped ominously around her, but she was stable in her sedation. She didn't know anything that was going on, and thankfully, she didn't seem to be in any pain. The surgery had stopped the bleeding and limited the damage to just the area already affected—we couldn't yet know how much that was.

Now, at her bedside, emotions swirled through my head. I felt both relief and terror. I felt pride that I had made tough decisions that had gotten her this far, from the airport to here. I also felt anger. How could this have happened to her? To us?

This would be a common place for my wandering thoughts to land in the months ahead.

It was about nine o'clock on one of the longest days of my life, and we were told there was nothing more we could do that night. As we gathered our things to leave for the evening, we saw Father K, the priest who had married us and a colleague of Kelly's, approaching us from down the hall.

Kelly's mom mentioned his resemblance to Clarence, the angel in *It's a Wonderful Life*.

I had no idea how he knew what had happened, but what a welcome sight he was. We chatted until about midnight, when everyone finally headed home. Kelly's sister, Katie, went home with me, ostensibly to help me unpack the New Orleans suitcase and put together a few things for the hospital stay.

I'm pretty sure they just didn't want me to be alone that night.

Although my adrenaline had slowed, my mind was still trying to make sense of the events of the day, and I doubted I'd get any sleep. I prayed harder and longer than ever before.

Kelly deserved all the prayers in the world that night, as much as she had done for others in her life. If anyone should benefit from God's grace, it was her.

As soon as my head hit the pillow, exhaustion overtook me. As I drifted off, I thought of Katie in the next room. Kelly and Katie had always been close and shared a bedroom for many years, and they believed in their special Bobbsey Twin powers to protect them, often from the antics of their brothers. I could imagine Katie invoking those powers as she tried to find sleep herself.

Kelly would like that, I thought to myself.

Generalized Trauma

Stepping into Kelly's hospital room again the next morning was a surreal experience. Her monitoring machines continuously whistled and beeped, and there was a steady hum of activity on the floor as staff tended to the patients and spoke quietly with other families.

Kelly was still heavily sedated but breathing on her own through a mask. Her head was almost entirely bandaged and covered. I could only see her right eye and part of her face, but it was so swollen from the trauma of surgery that she looked nothing like herself.

Seeing her lying there so still and helpless, I was rocked by another wave of disbelief that this could have happened to us. *What must she be thinking? Is she in pain?* I wondered. *If only I could switch places with her, I would do that in a heartbeat.*

In our morning consultation, the doctors explained that when the brain swells, it moves off-center in the skull. The more it shifts, the less it works.

As with any injury, blood had rushed to Kelly's brain in an effort to heal it. But because the excess blood had nowhere to go, it had collected, killing more brain cells every minute. That was why the surgeons had performed a craniotomy and why they would leave the piece of skull off for up to twelve weeks—to allow room for the brain to swell naturally. In the meantime, sedation would hopefully keep her comfortable and quiet.

About eighteen months later, in January 2011, we would all hear about a similar situation in great detail as the nation watched Senator Gabby Giffords of Arizona recover from a gunshot wound to the head sustained during a public appearance at a shopping mall. Although the causes of their injuries were different, Kelly and Ms. Giffords would follow eerily similar paths to recovery from their brain injuries.

Kelly's bed was just one of ten or so in a large room filled with other trauma patients. Over there was a severed leg. On the other side was a bad heart. All kinds of other injuries and maladies existed in between, some routine and some disturbing. Nurses and doctors came and went, as did family members of the afflicted.

There was no room for me to hang around without getting in the way, so I went back through the double doors into the waiting room with the family. Kelly's brother Rob was there with his wife, Keri. Rob is a nurse, and Keri worked for a prominent local doctor, so they were our family medical experts, helping me fill in the blanks and make decisions whenever the explanations from the doctors were unclear to me. Without their help, I would have had to go on the Internet on an hourly basis for help in translating all the medical and pharmacological terms.

"I've been thinking," Rob said, "that it would be better if we could move Kelly to a unit that is focused on neurology. The emergency care here has been great, but it doesn't make sense to keep her in a generalized trauma ICU."

We took this idea to Kelly's surgeon, along with our questions about the risks and benefits of moving her.

"She is recovering, and we can certainly take care of her here," he told us. "But given her situation, I could understand if you wanted to move her to a neural ICU if available." He proceeded as carefully as he had before, saying, "I can't tell you what to do. It's up to you."

Of course it is, I thought, but I got the message behind his whitewashed words. It's helpful to understand that most of the specialists or surgeons in hospitals are part of private practice groups, so while they have an allegiance to the hospital, they likely practice elsewhere and know that not all facilities are created equal or have the right focus for a particular patient's needs. In our case, his nonverbal cues as he spoke told me what I needed to know: she needed focused care from neural specialists if we could find a way to get it. I had no way to know how smart this decision would be until the days to come.

So Rob went to work trying to figure out if there was a way to have her admitted to the local university medical center, which was equipped with a neurospecific ICU. Working his contacts, he was able to get us a bed there in only a matter of hours—a major coup, especially on short notice. We got the go-ahead in the late afternoon and started the paperwork for the transfer.

Little did I know I would learn a lifetime of lessons about health care red tape over the coming months.

While we were waiting for everything to go through, family and friends continued to gather. My parents had arrived earlier in the day, and my brother Casey had flown in on the first flight he could get from New Jersey.

We took turns being with Kelly, watching closely for signs of progress or pain. Every once in a while, she would move around and open her right eye as much as she could. It seemed she was trying to communicate—that she was nodding, that her head hurt. She was wiggling her toes.

I took every single movement to mean that she was recognizing us and trying to tell us something. In reality, she was so doped up that those movements were not purposeful movements; they were involuntary reflexes. However, I was desperate for a sign—any sign—that my wife was still in there.

In times like this, people need hope, encouragement, and faith, because nothing good happens fast, and all you have is time to imagine the worst. I was no different, and Kelly's family tried to help themselves and me pass the time with one particular story about her grandpa.

Years ago, a psychic had told Kelly's aunt Kris that if she found a penny, it was a sign that Kelly's late grandpa Davies was thinking of them. It used to infuriate Grandpa when someone would not take the time or energy to pick up a penny, as if it weren't really money.

On that Monday morning, we received the first of many pennies from heaven. First, Kelly's sister-in-law Mindy picked up a magazine, and a penny fell out from the pages. Then a man stood up, and a penny fell from his lap, rolled toward us, and landed at our feet. We took these incidents as sure signs that Grandpa Davies was looking out for Kelly and for all of us.

In spite of my desperation, I wasn't sure that the pennies were a sign of anything, but I believed Kelly would think so, and at that point, I was glad for any encouragement I could get.

Everyone started keeping his or her eyes out for stray pennies, and soon we had a jar full of pennies. Grandpa Davies would continue to send us these good vibrations throughout the next forty-seven days.

The Undiagnosis

It is a surreal feeling to see an ambulance on the highway and know your loved one is inside. About five o'clock that Monday afternoon, not even twenty-four hours after her surgery, Kelly was taken by ambulance to the university hospital. This time, I did not beat her there, which was encouraging.

I watched as an entire team of neurofocused doctors—some specializing in blood work, some in radiology, and some in seizures—met Kelly at the door. The VIP treatment made it clear that we had a team now, and I immediately knew we were in the right place. It had been a gamble to move her, but it clearly had been the right call.

While she was in a not-quite-private room, Kelly had her own area with a curtain and a chair, so I could sit beside her for as long as I wanted. When I saw her for the first time, the monitors were already up and running. Their now-familiar beeps and hums were becoming white noise, the everyday sounds one hears but pays no attention to.

They took her to radiology right away and repeated all the tests she had been having—MRIs, CAT scans, etc. The goal, other than keeping her stabilized, was to figure out what had caused the bleed so that they could prevent it from recurring.

The good news was that the surgery had stopped the bleeding, and the bleeding had not restarted. The bad news, at least from our perspective, was that they still didn't know why or how it had happened.

It was after this round of tests that a doctor finally used the word *stroke* to describe what had happened to Kelly. It had been a hemorrhagic stroke, to be precise. I had always thought a stroke was more or less a mini–heart attack. How naive I had been.

According to the specialist, out of the 750,000 strokes that happen each year in the United States, approximately 90 percent are ischemic strokes, which are caused by a blockage of an artery, similar to the way a blockage in a coronary artery will cause a heart attack. The remaining 10 percent are hemorrhagic—in other words, a bleed. While the symptoms are typically similar, the events are very different.

In the event of an ischemic stroke, the damage is usually limited to the part of the brain that is deprived of oxygen. Although an ischemic stroke can be fatal, if the victim gets to the doctor quickly, he or she can often recover fully. Ischemic strokes have both a hereditary component and lifestyle components, so even after making dietary changes and getting more exercise, a person who has one is still at high risk of having another.

A hemorrhagic stroke typically occurs when there's a preexisting condition or risk factor, such as an aneurysm or a traumatic brain injury. Of all hemorrhagic strokes, 20 percent (and even a higher percentage in young women) fall into the spontaneous category. There's no aneurysm or systemic cause to be found; they just happen. One or more blood vessels weaken and eventually burst, and there is no way of telling what the trigger might have been.

"The good news," the doctor explained, "is that people who suffer spontaneous hemorrhagic strokes, as it appears Kelly has, have only a slightly greater chance of having another one than you or I."

In the case of spontaneous hemorrhagic strokes, the closest term doctors can give to explain the cause is vasculitis, a disease of the blood vessels in which they're weaker than they ought to be. Over time, vasculitis becomes a significant risk factor for a stroke.

"Had Kelly been having any unusual symptoms in recent months?" her doctor asked me.

I considered this. I had already been racking my brain for signals I might have missed leading up to her illness. "Now that you mention it, we noticed that Kelly seemed to be more susceptible to alcohol lately. It seemed like she would have one glass of wine and suddenly be significantly affected by it. She was starting to have these headaches too, which was unusual for her. A couple of times, she didn't remember things, which we thought was sort of weird. But we thought all of it was just stress. Could those be symptoms?"

"Possibly," he said, and he began to run down his list of possible causes and risk factors for vasculitis among young women.

"Birth control pills," he said. Kelly had taken birth control pills at one time, but it had been a few years since she'd stopped.

"Smoking can also thin the blood vessels." Kelly smoked socially, maybe one or two cigarettes a day. We used to joke that she invented the two-puff cigarette, because she would light a cigarette, take two puffs, and then be done with it. We teased her about what a waste of money that was.

"Other studies point to pseudoephedrine, which is a decongestant. That's the ingredient they sell behind the pharmacy counter now because it's used to make crystal meth." At her doctor's recommendation, Kelly had taken a decongestant every day for a long time for her allergies.

Then came an uncomfortable moment. "Did Kelly possibly have a cocaine addiction?"

What do you mean?

"Did she have any drug addictions—cocaine, methamphetamine?" he clarified.

I answered automatically, "No, of course not."

That didn't stop him from asking again. Like Dr. House, he was just doing his job, but I didn't appreciate the insinuation that my wife had some secret drug-addicted life I didn't know about.

As he kept after me, there was a split second when I thought, *I travel a lot. Maybe there's something I didn't know about.*

Katie was standing beside me. She and Kelly were, after all, the inseparable Bobbsey Twins, best friends who worked out together three days a week and talked on the phone every night. It wasn't as if Kelly was by herself all the time when I was out of town. In fact, she was rarely alone. I looked at Katie, who answered my unasked question emphatically: "Absolutely not."

My experience with the medical establishment up to that point in my life had been limited to a yearly checkup (or one every three years), visits with elders who had typical situations somewhat expected with old age, and the occasional medical drama on television, in which the doctor always diagnoses the problem just in time. It had never occurred to me that the doctors wouldn't be able to tell us why the stroke had happened—that there wouldn't be an underlying cause we could identify and address.

I wouldn't say I got angry, but the drug discussion pushed some buttons. I thought to myself, *Why don't you focus on figuring this out instead of trying to find an easy explanation just because you don't have a medical one?*

The truth was that there was no easy explanation. Kelly had some of the risk factors, but so did half the female population. There were no big red flags, and there was nothing the doctors could pinpoint as the cause.

Regardless, it didn't make any difference now. In the aftermath of a spontaneous hemorrhagic stroke, auto accident, bad fall, or gunshot, the reality is similar. The cause, known or unknown, was in the past, and we needed to focus on the future.

"So now what?" I asked.

"Well, the other major challenge with a hemorrhagic stroke is that it has a fifty percent mortality rate in the first two weeks because the blood spreads so quickly throughout the brain and is much more toxic than oxygen deprivation. Blood kills brain tissue everywhere it touches."

"Wait," I said, stopping him. "So the danger hasn't really passed?"

"We don't know the extent of the damage to her brain yet, and her condition could worsen before it improves." He held up the MRI results, which looked like a dental or bone x-ray image, with the white light behind it highlighting the lobes of Kelly's brain. I had never seen an MRI, but I learned quickly that in this case, shadows were bad news. Shadows on an MRI mean damaged areas, just as a cavity shows up on a dental x-ray, and in Kelly's case, they were apparent. "We can see from this that the blood has reached all three lobes of her brain. The shadows you see here," he said, pointing at the image, "represent damage caused by blood permeating brain tissue where it's not supposed to be."

My heart sank as a new awareness dawned. I could see the huge shaded areas on the MRI; there were shadows everywhere, it seemed. My mind quickly jumped to a vision of Kelly in a wheelchair, or worse, before I pulled my thoughts back to the discussion. "So is she going to be okay?" I asked.

"We simply can't give you a prognosis for recovery. We're hopeful. We've stopped the bleeding, and she's stable for the moment. She will likely have damage to her physical, cognitive, and communication abilities, but we won't know until she gets out of the ICU."

Every stroke affects the brain differently, depending on the areas damaged. There could be problems controlling movements or strength, trouble with fine motor skills, sensory issues, difficulty with memory, and difficulty with using and understanding language and speaking. Typically, damage cannot be assessed until after the brain swelling has gone down and the patient has stabilized, but you hope that the damage is isolated to one part of the brain so that the individual's chance of full recovery is maximized. This is why ischemic stroke survivors can sometimes recover much more of their faculties than hemorrhagic stroke survivors. The lack of oxygen is often focused in one area as opposed to a bleed that kills cells as quickly as it spreads in multiple areas. Kelly had drawn a bad hand for sure, but I was still hopeful.

"So now what?" I asked for what felt like the hundredth time in just two days.

"Now we wait."

If We Only Knew: Awareness and Advocacy

- There are two types of strokes: ischemic strokes, which are caused by a blood clot, and hemorrhagic. While the symptoms are typically similar, they are different types of strokes with different effects and causes.

- There were signs we should have had checked out, including severe and recurring headaches, anxiety, fatigue, and an increased susceptibility to alcohol. If you have these symptoms, go to the ER or see your physician as soon as possible.

- There are activities and medicines correlated with stroke in young women. Taking birth control, taking pseudoephedrine, and smoking over many years are all possible risk factors.

- Now is the time to get legal guardianship and power of attorney in place in case you need it. The courts take too long, and HIPAA rules make it difficult to access necessary insurance, medical, and financial accounts for the survivor if you don't already have joint accounts. It is likely even more difficult for nonspousal situations. Ask about options in your state from your attorney.

- Consider that a stroke requires neurological care, and if your hospital is like the first hospital we went to, it won't have the specialized care that can make such a difference. We were lucky in that we had someone who had contacts to get the care we needed, but you might not have that. It's best to ask for the neurological care facility when the ambulance comes. However, if you can't get to a hospital that offers neurological care, you can ask the nurses, doctors, hospital social workers, and anyone else you come in contact with if they have any recommendations. You can always call the customer service line for the insurance company and ask them to recommend a hospital with neurological care. Some companies also employ a health advocate to help you navigate the health care system, and you might be able to contact one as part of your benefits. You can also read up on this topic before you need to use this information. Sites like USNews.com rank hospitals based on neurology and neurosurgery. The links are in the list of website resources at the end of the book.

- Despite the stress of the situation, be patient and respectful but squeaky with hospital staff. As the saying goes, the squeaky wheel gets the oil, but that is true only if you follow their rules and make it apparent you are simply representing the voice of the patient, who cannot speak for him- or herself.

CHAPTER 3

It's Called Intensive for a Reason

Brad

We settled into the neurological intensive care unit and quickly learned the new rules and regulations that would govern our life in the coming days. Visiting hours were from 11:00 a.m. to 1:00 p.m. and from 4:00 p.m. to 7:00 p.m., with a limit of two visitors in her room at a time.

As inconvenient as the hours were, everyone still assembled daily to keep the vigil; none of Kelly's close family could even think about going to work. My brother stayed with me for a week before returning to New Jersey. Friends were calling me to find out what was going on, and people were showing up for visiting hours.

Both wings of the neuro ICU were filled to capacity and shared a small waiting room, so the Marsh and Rickenbaugh clan was packed in there tightly. At that stage, only the immediate family members were allowed in Kelly's room, but that didn't keep other family and friends from dropping by to offer their support.

We shared the waiting room with three or four other families, all keeping vigils for loved ones in disastrous situations. We saw them come and go and watched with heartache the many who did not receive the good news they were hoping for.

I specifically remember the family of a child who had been hit by a car. He was admitted early in the week, and we watched his family gather, funnel back for visiting hours, comfort one another, and cry together. We saw the nurse come get the family and escort them back to a private room to share the worst of all possible news. We watched that whole process and tried not to imagine being in their shoes. Then a new family would appear, and the cycle would repeat with varying outcomes. It's an oddly depressing yet high-energy place.

Still, we knew it was better than the alternative.

In the hospital world, I'm sure there are high-maintenance family members and low-maintenance family members. I strove to be on the low-maintenance side; I did not want to get in the staff's way, cause any problems, or irritate or aggravate Kelly. That way, they would let me stay later in the evening. I discovered that if you're actually supporting the patient instead of agitating the staff, the nurses would rather have you there than not. I spent most of my time in the room with her, leaving only when they needed to bathe her or take her for more tests.

Occasionally, I would have to lobby on Kelly's behalf. They still only had half her head shaved, and I knew she would have hated that, so I asked if they could shave the other half. They wouldn't do it, but she had other grooming needs that someone needed to take care of, which I pointed out to the staff. I asked them to please shave her legs and to put some pajama bottoms on her.

Dignity is important, even in desperate times.

Daily MRI scans tracked whether the swelling in Kelly's brain had started to subside and whether her brain had begun to move back into place. That was the sign we were all looking for to signal the beginning of her recovery.

Like any family in a tough situation, we were on the lookout for any positive signs we could get. "I had a dream last night," Rob said one morning. "I was sitting on a bench, and a man came by and sat down next to me. He told me, 'Rob, your whole life has been built up to this moment in time. Your choices in leaving your job in manufacturing, going to nursing school, walking away from the job at the hospital, and even pursuing the random jobs that didn't work out eventually led you to the doctor's office you work in now. All these experiences prepared you for this opportunity to help your sister.'"

We embraced Rob's dream, because his expertise and connections in the nursing and medical fields gave us greater peace of mind and enabled us to get better treatment and attention for Kelly. He was asking all the right questions and translating the answers from medical jargon to plain English for us.

I don't know what kind of care or attention we would have received if it were not for Rob being there right by my side as a sounding board. He was Kelly's health advocate, and he knew more about medicine and the ins and outs of the health care system than anyone else in the family. It was a big help to me to have someone knowledgeable to confirm my decisions.

Kelly was spending the better part of each day medicated and sleeping. Even when she appeared awake, she was heavily sedated and easily agitated and disturbed, so we all tried our best not to overstimulate her. They tied down her left arm and leg, but still, she kept pulling herself up and lifting her body off the bed. We worried that she would hurt herself.

Then we joked that the new event for next year's Rickenfest, the family Olympics, would be to arm wrestle Kelly with her right hand tied behind her back. We chose to see it as a sign of her determination and will to fight.

Her nieces and nephews made cards for her, and for good luck, Rob brought some of Grandma Rickenbaugh's religious statues for the room. Kelly's mom and dad had a different idea for affecting her fortune: food for the staff.

Father K came by late one afternoon, and I offered to see if the staff might break the immediate-family-only rule and let him back to see Kelly. He just smiled at me, tapped his clerical collar, and replied with a wink, "This pretty much gets me into wherever I want to go."

It was one of my few laughs during those early weeks.

Staying Connected to the Outside World

A couple of days into Kelly's stay in the neuro ICU, we discovered the online CarePages, web pages offered for free by the hospital, and we signed up right away. We were already having trouble fielding all the calls and e-mails coming in from Kelly's extensive network of family, friends, and colleagues, so an electronic updating system sounded great to us. Most hospitals offer this kind of social community now, but it was still pretty new at the time. It was such a great help and time-saver for us because we could give one update to many people, freeing up time.

Katie and I spent lots of time writing Kelly's story and sharing updates on her condition. Kelly wasn't allowed to have flowers or cards in her room, and we soon found out that many people were starting and ending their days by logging on to the CarePages and leaving messages for all of us in lieu of cards.

We tried to keep the posts general and not get into the weeds with too much medical detail. After all, we had been getting new information every day, so not everything we initially wrote turned out to be accurate. We were more upbeat and positive on the CarePage than we actually felt. We were putting on our brave faces, as this post shows:

> Tuesday, September 1, 2009, 2:59 p.m.
>
> Kelly continues to make gains! She is opening her eyes when she hears her name and looking around for who is saying it. Her eyes have stayed the same, which is a really good sign. When asked if her head hurt, she was able to nod yes. She also wiggled her toes on both sides. She does not have a lot of movement on her right side (surgery was on the left). On Monday, she said two three-word sentences to Brad.
>
> We know that Kelly is a fighter and will be able to conquer the long road to recovery ahead. Contrary to popular belief, this was not caused by Kelly's clumsy and klutzy ways that always lead to her many falls and stumbles.
>
> We are praying and keeping our fingers crossed; please continue to do the same.
>
> Thank you for all of your thoughts and prayers. We will keep everyone posted.
>
> LYMI,
>
> Marshes and Rickenbaughs

We signed every post with that family acronym, which stands for "Love you. Mean it."

A Test of Patience

When will Kelly be conscious? When will I know the extent of the damage? I had many questions, but there were no answers.

"Nothing good happens fast in the ICU," the staff would say when I pressed them. "Just wait. That's all we can do now."

I had never been a very religious person. In fact, that had been the big debate during our six-year courtship. But something happened to me during that first week. I began to understand faith and to feel the presence of a higher power in a way I never had before. Nightly, I begged for her to have a chance to come back from this.

At the hospital, I was all business, but when I was at home, I was overcome with a mixture of feelings—disbelief, sadness, concern.

There are plenty of books and even pamphlets from the hospital discussing the survivors' likely stages of grief, which include denial, anger, bargaining, and acceptance, but the materials don't really address the caregivers, who will experience the same emotional stages but have to put their feelings on hold to be their loved ones' advocates and voices. Understanding and dealing with these emotional changes and losses are just as important as the physical issues that are dealt with in the rehabilitation process.

One night I took one of Kelly's favorite sets of pajamas out of her drawer and put it on the bed. I just laid it out as if she were there.

So as painful as it was for me to hear at the time that nothing good happens fast in the ICU, years later, I found myself using those exact words to comfort friends with ill family members.

While I'd started sleeping at home again, I was back at the hospital first thing every morning. My priorities were the following: trying to figure out what happened, trying to make sure the doctors and hospital staff were on top of things, trying to make sure her family and I were doing everything we could to get to the next stage, and then keeping people updated on that information.

I connected my laptop wherever I could and took meetings by phone or in the cafeteria, wherever I could get a signal. I stayed late into the evening, until they asked me to leave, and came back first thing in the morning. I made a point of knowing all the nurses and doctors by name, and I took notes in every meeting with doctors so that I could remember the many tests and medications.

"Brad," Katie told me, "you really are her Superman."

"I'm just trying to get through this," I said, "and doing what any good husband would do."

If I had just been the husband I was only a few days earlier, I might have been counting on the hospital staff or doctors to take the lead on Kelly's care, but this guy taking charge was Kelly's new life manager, and he was quickly becoming an expert.

Life manager is the only term I can think of to describe the transformation of my existence and motivation within twenty-four hours to being more about someone else than myself. Kelly needed an advocate and a voice to proactively ask the right questions and make her life decisions to deliver the best chance of recovery while she was unable to speak and decide for herself. Making these choices and being accountable for the person is more of a commitment than most people experience and appreciate until later in life, and I was learning it as I went. For stroke survivors, having a committed caregiver is particularly important, as the survivors often have communication challenges along with physical challenges, so they are unable to help themselves. My personal observation is that there are a lot of people in hospitals every day whose families are not up to that job, and the result can be a much lower ceiling for their recovery and future independence.

The fact is, severe depression is also a serious risk for both the survivor and the caregiver. As a caregiver, there is so much pressure to take it all in and understand what is happening to make the best decisions you can. That stress, along with inadequate financial or health care resources, likely overwhelms many well-intended caregivers. We were lucky to have a great support network and better resources than most. Still, those were some of the toughest days and nights I hope I ever experience.

No Guarantees

Those first days in the ICU were relatively calm. We hung out in the waiting room every day, drinking cheap coffee and eating out of vending machines. We took turns going back to see Kelly. She often appeared to be awake and alert, and we convinced ourselves that this was the case, because we badly needed to believe it was.

Sometimes she would move around and grip with her left hand, as if she were trying to climb out of bed. We touted it on her CarePage as an illustration of what a fighter she was. Realistically, the gripping and other movements were mostly involuntary and meant little. Worse, we still had seen no movement on her right side, which had been affected by the damage to the left side of her brain.

Then, one morning, out of the blue, our cautious optimism was shattered when she started having seizures.

Here we go, I thought. The doctors had warned me about the 50 percent mortality rate in the first two weeks. *We could use a break,* I pleaded to the man upstairs. *She deserves a break. It's her turn for some luck.*

"One in four people in Kelly's situation starts to have these seizures as the brain swells to heal," one doctor explained. "It's just her brain reacting to what's happened and freaking out. That is what you were seeing when her arm and leg twitched and tremored before the surgery."

That made sense to me. Her always-on, type-A brain was frantically trying to figure out how to fix everything. Some of its pathways were blocked, so it just started firing signals everywhere to figure out new ways to get things to work. This was a normal defense mechanism at exactly the wrong time. What we really needed was for her brain to be quiet.

The doctors ordered heavy sedation to calm her whole body, particularly her brain. "We've maxed out on her Versed dosage," one told us. "That is enough sedative to knock out most men twice her size."

Kelly's eyes remained open, and the seizures continued.

The hours, and then days, crept by as the doctors gave us milestones and medication targets. I kept a log of every medication, dosage, and target. "If she goes twelve hours with no seizures, then we can drop the dosage of this medication," one of the doctors told me. However, for a few days, the medications were only being increased. Nothing seemed to work.

The neurologist consulted an epilepsy specialist to determine if they should increase the medicine slightly, and soon she was on three different seizure medicines, all at the maximum dosage. The doctors warned us that if she needed an even higher dosage, she wouldn't be able to breathe on her own. As I later learned, that would have meant a medically induced coma and life support.

The seizure specialist was monitoring Kelly's EEG continuously, even from home at night, on monitors next to her bed. Talk about commitment! I think I might have jokingly asked if they could give me electronic access from home so that I could watch Kelly's EEG too, not that I knew how to read it. With seizures, blips are bad, and flat lines are good. *Go figure.*

Needless to say, no log-in was granted.

Meanwhile, the heavy sedation did eventually lead to Kelly's inability to breathe on her own, and when the mask stopped working, they had to perform a tracheotomy. She was also asleep long enough that they had to insert a PEG tube into her stomach to feed her. That was a tough conversation.

Still, the seizures continued. We were getting dangerously close to the medically induced coma, although she was basically on life support already.

I asked every doctor and nurse who entered her room, "How long will it take before the seizures stop? How long until the swelling in her brain subsides?"

The answer was always the same: "Brad, nothing good happens fast in the ICU. Just be patient. Time is what it's going to take. Keep doing what you're doing."

But I wasn't doing anything, and that was what was killing me. I was helpless; we were all helpless. I had never been in a situation I could not control or at least influence. There was truly nothing to do but wait, hope, and have faith.

One afternoon in the waiting room, Kelly's brother Jamie saw another penny from heaven to add to our growing collection. However, before he could reach it, another guy picked it up. "He doesn't know it doesn't belong to him—that it was meant for us," Jamie said.

What did this mean? Was this a bad sign that other people were picking up our pennies?

Even the least superstitious people look for any positive signs in times of crisis. While I knew how grave the situation was with the seizure activity and possible induced coma, it would only have raised more questions and made things more hectic to communicate that level of detail to friends and family. We knew that fielding the e-mails and calls of concern would be overwhelming at this stage. If we needed to provide more-extensive details later, we would, but for now, I wanted to add some levity to the CarePages posts—for me and for everyone following our progress. The following post drew rave reviews.

Thursday, September 3, 2009, 2:22 p.m.

Kelly has generated quite a social community, and all the thoughts and prayers are helping her (and us) get through the day, so keep them coming. In fact, her nurse asked us to post an update so she wouldn't have to continue to screen calls in the ICU.

Wednesday was focused on getting seizure activity under control. Her brain fighting to function is typically a great thing, but when what we need is for it to relax, it's not so beneficial. Her CT scan from Wednesday night showed no change since Monday, meaning swelling has not worsened, and the blood levels have not increased. All good news. We need the next CT to show decreased swelling and blood levels. That would be a leading indicator that we might be turning the corner. Until then, it will be a day-by-day adventure.

To change the tone of the update a little, I thought I would share the top ten quotes from the ICU staff that characterize our star:

1) Nice toenail polish. Does she do her own nails?
2) Boy, her nieces and nephews sure can color good.
3) What I've learned today is that this little girl can take a <u>lot</u> of medicine, and she's still awake!
4) She's beautiful.
5) She kept me on my toes all night.
6) She's a fighter.
7) I wouldn't have guessed she was thirty-six; she looks so young.

8) 553 kilograms—I haven't weighed that since high school.
9) So much for that restraint. Get me another.
10) Maybe if we put wine in the IV, she would cooperate.
11) (Okay, that last one wasn't a nurse.)

Hail Mary

Labor Day weekend was business as usual in the NSICU at the university hospital. The last hurrah of summer meant little to us. We were desperate to stop the seizure activity.

"We're down to our final option," one of the doctors told me. "Even our highest levels of medication have not halted the seizure activity. We need to place Kelly in an induced coma."

"For how long?" I asked.

"The shortest amount of time possible—no longer than twenty-four to thirty-six hours. The risks of an induced coma over a longer period of time are high. There is a risk she will not come out of it."

"So what if the coma doesn't work? What is the next step then?"

"I'm afraid there is no next step," the doctor replied. "This is a last-ditch effort to stop the seizure activity."

We were moving backward, and it was completely out of my hands. This sent me reeling emotionally. I shared the news with the family, and we doubled down on our prayers.

I worked hard to stay strong for them, but later, when I found some time alone, I could only break down and beg whoever was listening to let her be okay.

Wishful Thinking

Miraculously, a few hours into the induced coma, Kelly's seizures began to subside.

Within twelve hours, they were below the critical threshold, slowly decreasing from one every five seconds to one every fifteen seconds and then every thirty seconds, five minutes, and, eventually, twenty-four hours. The seizures were no longer systemic, and we heaved huge sighs of relief that our prayers had been answered.

With the seizures under control, the doctors slowly reduced the seizure medications, bringing her out of the induced coma. "We have to watch closely while we drop the dosage," one doctor warned us. "So far, the medication has been keeping the seizures at bay. Now we have to see if she can hold them off on her own."

They cut her bandages back so that we could see both eyes, and the swelling had subsided enough that she looked like herself, even though she was black and blue. Her brain was shifting back to its proper alignment, and they were reducing the dose of her pain medication.

As she regained consciousness and opened her eyes, we searched for signs that she was recognizing voices and faces. She couldn't speak at this point, so we didn't know what, if any, cognitive deficits she might have. We believed we were seeing signs of her old self, her feisty personality, in her eyes.

I warned the nursing staff, "Once she really wakes up, you guys are in for it. She is going to be a handful!"

It was a bit of wishful thinking, I guess, but the current situation was certainly better than when she was not moving and not awake at all or opening her eyes, because it showed that those muscles and nerves worked.

For a little while one Saturday morning, Kelly was able to breathe without the ventilator, but soon she developed swelling in her throat and a cough or cold, which prevented her from breathing or swallowing on her own. So back on the ventilator she went, along with a dosage of steroids for the throat swelling. We worried about how much of this trauma Kelly would remember when she woke up. To our relief, her doctors reassured us that she likely wouldn't remember any of it.

Kelly was sleeping again, and our focus moved to hoping that her brain continued to heal, in addition to her cough and throat swelling dissipating. If she could improve in both these areas, they would remove the ventilator, and we would be on our way to rehab.

In spite of the continuing roller coaster, we felt we truly had something for which to be grateful. The seizures were under control and seemed to be a hurdle we had cleared.

A special mass was planned for Kelly the Saturday before Labor Day. It was a gorgeous late-summer day; the humid haze had lifted, and the sun burned in the perfectly clear blue sky. It was the first time I had been anywhere but the hospital or home in a week.

More than a hundred people attended, including all the aunts, uncles, and cousins; several of Kelly's coworkers; and even some of her friends from high school. We were amazed that so many people would gather in the middle of a holiday weekend to pray for Kelly. We had asked those who could not attend from all over the world to pause for a moment of prayer at 5:00 p.m. that day. After the mass, the priest held a special healing prayer service for us in the rear of the church. I also received e-mails from out-of-town colleagues and friends who were thinking of Kelly that day. She had touched a lot of people.

Our week of hell was coming to a close, and I was beginning to feel as if I could breathe again.

On Labor Day, I relented and gave Kelly's life manager a half day off. We decided to hold the family fantasy football draft that had been scheduled for the day of the stroke. We drank a few beers, talked football, and tried to forget for just a few minutes what was going on.

I thought back to the team Kelly and I had discussed on our flight from New Orleans to Cincinnati, trying to remember the players she had wanted on our team. I had a feeling she would still want to watch football when she woke up, so I was even more committed to drafting the team she had chosen. The draft was a nice distraction, and other than Kelly's absence, it felt like a few normal hours from our previous life.

Except that she wasn't there.

Still, Kelly's family convinced me that she would have wanted me to take a break and try to relax, so I went with a friend to the annual Labor Day fireworks gathering on the river.

As I watched the elaborate fireworks display that Kelly and I had attended together in past years, I realized that it just wasn't the same. While I knew it was important for my mental state to try to take a break, nothing was the same without Kelly. She had to get better, and I desperately wanted her back.

If We Only Knew: ICU 101

- "Nothing good happens fast in the ICU." This saying could not be truer, so as difficult as it might be, you have to be patient and keep a clear head. You will receive a lot of technical information to digest and could have to make an important decision any minute.

- Get to know the staff. They can seem cold and matter-of-fact at times, but remember, they cannot get attached to patients. By definition, they have to stay objective, follow protocol, and be prepared to communicate the worst of news. That said, they are human and react positively to seeing supportive and caring family members. They will bend the rules on visitation and sharing information if they know you will not take advantage of it.

- Get to know your insurance provider's agents by name if possible, and ask for direct contact information and emergency contact options so that you don't have to go through the call system. The insurance workers are people too and can sympathize with caregivers more than the doctors, so try to build a rapport.

- The ICU will assign a caseworker to help you with many aspects of care, including navigating the hospital and identifying options for what happens after the ICU. Seek out your caseworker proactively to discuss and plan options.

- Make use of social media and Internet resources. During the many hours of waiting, use social media to keep friends and family up to date so that you don't have to repeat the same information to different people.

- You will be digesting a lot of new information and medical jargon. Do research online to make sure you understand it. You might find it helpful to write things down and keep all the information together in a folder. The ICU usually assigns a caseworker to help you, so be sure to ask if you have any questions. If you have a family member you trust who works in the medical field, ask him or her to help you. Information makes a big difference, and good information can make all the difference. People often hold those keys, so try to find them when you can.

- Start planning for the next step. Assuming you are making progress, rehabilitation will be the next step, so you need to talk to your caseworker to understand options based on insurance, likely status of your loved one, and facilities available (or in-home care, if applicable).

CHAPTER 4

They Don't Mess around in Rehab

With Kelly's seizures under control and the steroids doing their work on her throat, it was time to begin planning for the next step: rehab.

Among all the options we had to consider, one stood above all the rest: a regional center for postacute care that we were lucky enough to have right in Cincinnati. As Kelly continued to recover, I took a drive with her parents, Kathie and Rick, to check it out.

It's important to realize that while *rehab* is a ubiquitous term, facilities are all different and range from the most general to more specialized to in-home options. The right choice depends on patient needs and care available in the region, and obviously, the patient's insurance and financial situation also weigh heavily on alternatives.

For stroke survivors, the right facility is likely based on the section(s) of the brain impacted most significantly. In Kelly's case, the bleed caused damage in all three lobes of her brain on the left side, which meant we would likely need speech, occupational, and physical therapy for her best shot at a maximum recovery. If she'd only needed one type of therapy, we might have made a different choice. We were fortunate that the major facilities under consideration accepted our insurance. Your ICU caseworker is a great resource for information and will do the initial legwork on your options based on the likely status of the patient and the other variables listed above. The caseworker should be assigned while you are in the ICU working toward recovery, and if one is not, you should ask your ICU doctor and nursing staff how to get one.

We knew rehab could be a slow and arduous process, so on our first visit to the rehab center, we were a little taken aback by how active the residents seemed to be. Of course, we couldn't know what stage each patient had reached with his or her recovery or what each person was recovering from. But as we saw the patients walking the halls of the facility and engaging in lively chatter with each other and the staff, we couldn't imagine Kelly being there anytime soon. I mean, she had just come out of a coma!

Still, there was no direction to go but forward. We took comfort in the glowing recommendations we heard from those who had been a part of rehabilitation at the center we visited, and we made the decision to apply for admission.

As we began preparations for her transfer, Kelly was removed from EEG monitoring and transitioned from IV-drip medication to oral medication administered through her PEG tube for pain and seizure control. Because she still had the tracheal tube in place, she would be admitted to the long-term acute care (LTAC) floor at the rehab facility, where she would stay until she could be removed from the ventilator.

A social worker on the ICU floor walked us through the red tape involved in the move to rehab. We were fortunate that our insurance was not the determining factor in how long Kelly could stay in ICU; many people are forced to move sooner. One thing I never understood was that the goal of the ICU is to get the patient out of the ICU, but to graduate and meet insurance requirements, you have to clear certain medical hurdles that likely make you less of a risk to regress. These might include breathing on your own, not having an infection, or having the ability to walk and care for yourself, depending on the facility.

While the patient's well-being is the priority, at times, you will feel helpless, waiting on people and the system to learn how to communicate. I would encourage you to also investigate options online and call your insurance company to talk to a patient representative to confirm your options. While the hospital staff will do everything they can, many times, the insurance company is more engaged when the patient calls. You can also check to see if the insurance company is missing information from the hospital that would expedite decisions and approvals. These details are the last thing you will want to think about while your loved one is trying to survive, but they are a necessary evil to get the best care.

We were ready to be done with the tragedy of the NSICU waiting room and the parade of brokenhearted families. In hindsight, I can say that if you ever want perspective on your problems, the waiting room at an ICU is a good place to get it. You realize pretty quickly how trivial your day-to-day worries are.

Once her fever broke, Kelly became more active during the day, although *active* is a relative term. She seemed to hear our voices but was unable to respond to commands, although we joked with the doctors that responding to commands had never been her specialty. She was always more of a command giver, but that was impossible with the tracheal tube in.

Vasculitis was now the top contender regarding the cause of Kelly's hemorrhagic stroke, though that was still just an educated guess after ruling out all other possible causes. The doctors prescribed a course of steroids to prevent another bleed during recovery.

Her latest CT scans showed a marked reduction in swelling, improvements in blood levels, and evidence of her brain shifting back toward center. Our hope was that as her brain resumed its rightful place, we would see improvements in her ability to clear her throat and swallow, which were the keys to getting her off the ventilator.

Approval to move to the rehab facility was a cause for celebration. In the meantime, Team Kelly's presence in the waiting room at the ICU began thinning out. It was time for everyone to go back to work and try to resume some semblance of a normal life.

The Support Network Grows

Late in the afternoon on September 11, just twelve days after suffering her stroke, Kelly made the journey from the hospital to the rehab facility. She—we—had beaten the two-week mortality odds.

A facility of that size is like a factory, and at first, we felt like cogs in a large machine. They have many patients and never enough staff. I was on pins and needles until we got to know the staff and they got to know her case.

It's no secret that nurses and health care aides are not in it for the money; they truly want to help people. But conditions can be tough, and like anybody else, they have rough days. Sometimes they take it out on the patients by using a stern tone in communication, rushing through their checklist, being a little rough in handling, not being available for assistance, or just not having the bedside manner they should. By and large, they are doing their best, and as I mentioned in the ICU chapters, the guidance I would give anybody is to try to build a relationship with the staff. Over time, we did. In the rare case that you do see or hear what you think is inappropriate care or behavior, don't be afraid to mention it to the senior administrator assigned to your case and ask for a change or at least ask him or her to investigate the situation.

Two factors are important in developing a good relationship. The first is a strong family support structure for a patient. A good support person listens to the doctors instead of arguing with them. I'm not saying doctors are always right, but if the support person has a productive patient-first attitude and tries to do what's required for the patient to get better, that is what the rehab staff wants to see. There are little things you can do too, such as bringing doughnuts and coffee, knowing the staff members' names and shifts, and asking about their families during downtime. It all adds up to better care for your loved one.

During my time in the rehab center, I saw many examples of people who did not have strong support. It can be scary in some cases, because as each patient's file grows thicker, there's no mechanism to guarantee that the staff will read everything. Important details can be missed if there isn't a family member present and prepared to intervene, such as dietary restrictions and allergies to certain medicines. Even if the information is all clearly in the file, it is not always reviewed by all staff. In my opinion, someone, preferably a consistently responsible family member, needs to be there during the major meetings with nurses and doctors the first week of rehab. This is especially true for patients who have speech limitations or who are still highly medicated for pain and therefore not lucid. Everyone will have a different system to stay prepared and remember everything that's coming at him or her, and there's a sample checklist in appendix B. Mine was pretty simple:

1. Document the names of all the doctors and their specialties, as well as next steps they tell you are in the plan for observation and treatment.

2. Ask if they are affiliated with a private group in addition to the hospital. Most are, and that is how scheduling happens and how you can get messages to them in addition to the nursing staff.
3. Document nurses' and nurse's aides' names and shifts so that you can share the information with other family.
4. Make sure you know all the medicines and what each is supposed to do.
5. Familiarize yourself with the testing and treatment that's happening (MRIs, CT, blood work, angiograms, craniotomies, cranioplasties, PEG tubes, AVM, ventilators, etc.).
6. Provide answers to questions about the patient and his or her allergies and preferences. Many people will ask you the same questions over and over again to form their own opinions of what the patient needs.
7. Know the visiting hours and daily schedule for medicine, personal needs, and doctors' check-in times. You don't want to show up and miss the doctor because he or she is in surgery and unavailable.

Seeing that a patient has a support structure and advocacy not only keeps the staff on their toes but also shows them that there are people invested in the patient's recovery besides them. It's not all on them to help the patient get to where he or she wants to go, and when it's finally time to go home, they feel reassured that all their good work won't go to waste.

The second factor in good relationships is the attitude of the patient. The staff reacts more positively to a patient who is willing to work hard and invest the time, energy, and heart to get better.

We saw a number of people who did not seem to want to recover. The staff had to cajole, argue, and even threaten them to get them to do their therapy. Many of those patients were elderly and perhaps had given up hope of regaining lost abilities. However, even some of the traumatic brain injury patients were subject to this. Patients would wake up in the facility and figure out where they were and why, and then the stages of grief would begin. I couldn't help but notice the disconnect between staff and patient until the patient truly accepted his or her situation and was prepared to deal with it.

I don't mean to sound ungrateful or judgmental. The staff does the best they can, but they don't always have the time or the resources to dig into the unique background of each patient and what makes each case different. I knew from our time at the NSICU that I would have to keep Get Kelly Back LLC open for business. I would have to be her advocate and her voice to be sure she got the treatment she needed, even at the best facility.

First Steps on the Road to Recovery

Kelly had become extremely alert and physically active since emerging from the induced coma. We were overjoyed to see such signs of life, but the downside was her persistence in trying to relieve any discomfort she felt from the IV or other equipment. Her IV was in her inactive right arm, but that left her good arm free to reach across and pull it out. That was why her left arm had been restrained at the ICU, but despite that note in her chart, that fact had not been communicated effectively to the rehab facility.

She was in a shared room for a few hours, and it became clear to me that they did not realize she still needed twenty-four-hour supervision. With all of her movement, her hospital gown was not enough to keep her covered, and she was often exposed for any passerby to see. Her catheter had also been removed, so she needed assistance to get in her wheelchair and go to the bathroom at night. She had always been a person who got up multiple times in the night to use the restroom, and that hadn't changed.

So my first battle on the first day of rehab was to secure a dedicated nurse's aide. Ensuring that Kelly had an aide was critical to my sanity, because I needed to be sure she was safe. I told them, "She needs someone in the room with her around the clock. She needs someone in there through the night to make sure she doesn't hurt herself and doesn't try to get up and walk. I'm not leaving her until there's someone in there watching her." The ICU staff had told me to request a nurse's aide at the rehab facility and said it should not be a problem, but the rehab facility seemed to assume the patient was fine without supervision until shown otherwise. I assumed cost was a factor in this predisposition, but I was not willing to wait until something bad enough happened to force them to allocate those resources. Before nightfall, my lobbying paid off, and she had twenty-four-hour nurse's aide supervision in place for her first night in rehab—not that she knew any of this. She was still in and out of consciousness, but I was able to go home that night.

Kelly explained to me months later that things can get a little scary through the night for a patient who cannot speak or is not independent to walk. After she got home, she described one situation when the nurse's aide sitting in her room—the sitter—was rude and threatening and spent more time on her phone in the middle of the night than assisting Kelly, who needed to get to the restroom a few times a night. This was one individual, but she was there most nights, and you can imagine how scary this would have been for someone in Kelly's condition, especially when rest and sleep were the most important things for her brain. I still think about how it must have felt for her to be all alone at night, unable to communicate or move parts of her body and unsure how it all happened. It must have been terrifying. Fortunately, this was the exception rather than the norm.

Within thirty-six hours of her arrival at the rehab facility, Kelly was off the ventilator and breathing on her own. The tracheal tube remained in her throat to help with clearing her lungs and for misting treatments.

She continued to have coughing fits, and during one of them, we saw her try to mouth some choice words. This was the first time since the surgery that we had seen her attempt to speak, and though she had no sound because of the tracheal tube, it was a major victory to see her try.

Kelly had picked up pneumonia in the ICU, and because of the amount of coughing she was doing to clear her lungs, it was too soon to put in the trachea plug that would allow her to talk. She communicated as much as she could without being able to speak. She mouthed words, made faces, and used her expressive eyes. The nurses were amazed at her progress in such a short period of time, but we could tell by now that Kelly was going to amaze them every step of the way.

Exactly two weeks after her stroke, we posted a truly joyful update:

Strength
September 13, 2009
Kelly smiled today!

She smiled several times that day and began to respond to questions with nods and head shakes. Her sister told her a story about a friend on the bus, and Kelly watched her through the whole story and then smiled and raised her eyebrow in understanding. These were more great signs.

We dared to hope that we were on the real road to recovery.

With Kelly out of immediate danger, I finally went back to work. Someone had left the company, and I had been asked to run a big meeting in his place.

"Do you think it's okay if I go to Minneapolis?" I asked Kelly's mom and dad, nervous about what they might think.

"Of course you need to go," her mom responded, to my relief. "Kelly is not in immediate danger. She's in good care, and we'll be here with her every day. You have been an absolute rock, Brad, but you need to take care of your job too."

So with mixed emotions, I left town on September 14, not realizing what excitement I would miss.

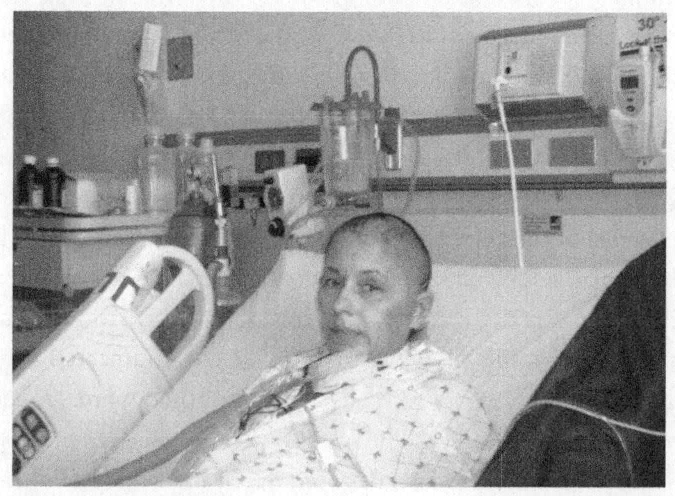

September 14, 2009, 7:35 p.m.
Extra! Extra! Read all about it!

Kelly's accomplishments for the day at rehab:

1) She crossed her right leg over her left leg. This is the first big "purposeful and controlled" movement we have seen on her right side!

2) She smiled at several people as they spoke to her!
3) She looked and smiled at Brad's mom, Connie, when she came to visit today!
4) She snarled at several people when she got mad at them!
5) She looked at people as they spoke to her and nodded her head yes or shook her head no to pictures and names we showed her!
6) She gave certain staff members what we call the "stink eye" when they spoke to her and moved her around and she was mad!
7) She kept her mom, Kathie, on her toes from eleven to three so that she could not sit down to finish her crossword puzzle!

Overall, another feisty and fabulous day of accomplishments at the rehab center! Keep those prayers and good thoughts coming; they all keep helping her make lots of gains!

LYMI,
Team Kelly

In the same way you remember exactly where you were when you heard about September 11, every detail of hearing that Kelly could move her right leg is etched in my memory. I had stepped away from a dinner meeting to call for the update, and it took me some time before I could dry my eyes enough to return to the table. Until then, we weren't sure if Kelly would have any movement in her right leg or arm, and Kathie was so excited that you would have thought Kelly had done a cartwheel.

Apparently, leaving town had been good luck.

Only one side of Kelly's head had been shaved, and her remaining hair had become a twisted, matted mess. Kathie knew Kelly would have hated that, so when one of the aides, Susan, offered to trim the other side, Kathie agreed, despite her hesitations about a health care worker's hairstyling skills. Her confidence was not helped when the aide came back with blunt-tipped scissors, but they were in it now.

Katie and Kathie had to lie across Kelly's body to hold her down while Susan snipped away at her hair. The growing collection of tangles on the pillow and Kelly's stubborn resistance to being groomed left her mom and sister nervous. But in the end, Susan proved to be more experienced at this than anyone would have guessed, and the blunt scissors did their job. Kelly was hardly runway ready, but the haircut was still a significant improvement.

Limitations

Kelly was fitted with a helmet, which she would have to wear when she was out of bed, to protect the part of her brain still exposed after the craniotomy. Then physical therapy could begin in a limited way, first by sitting her up in a specialized chair.

It was truly the Mercedes-Benz of wheelchairs, with hydraulics and special pedals and grips so that she could be easily lifted in and out. Kelly's family reported that she seemed to enjoy finally getting out of the bed, but she started to get overstimulated, so they thought it best to put her back in bed. To start, she was active for about thirty minutes at a time.

She also began speech and language therapy. After the first session, the therapist told us, "Kelly was able to nod her head yes or shake her head no to questions and get them right. I asked if she was in a church, and Kelly shook her head no. Then I asked if she was in the hospital, and she nodded yes. I asked if she knew what had happened to her, and she said no. So I tried to explain it to her, but I'm not sure she understood."

There were days when Kelly was active—or, as we described her in the CarePages, feisty. That was our nice way of describing her high level of agitation, which included pulling the tubes out of her body, slamming her fist on the bed, and trying to climb out of bed.

After enduring a few of these outbursts, the rehab staff mentioned that this could be due to overstimulation. "The noise and the people in her room are agitating her," one staff member told us. "She still needs to rest to let her brain recover and rejuvenate as much as possible. We recommend that she have no more than two people in her room at a time, and while you are in her room, don't talk, even to each other, unless she looks at you with questioning eyes. Then have one person respond in a very low, soothing voice."

Katie and Kelly's parents were surprised to hear this and wondered why this hadn't been made clear from the start in rehab. When I stepped away from my work dinner and called to check in from the road, Katie said, "Brad, we've been doing it all wrong. Why didn't they tell us? We've been just acting like our normal selves, with everyone in her face, talking all at once and making fast movements. Why didn't they tell us this was more than she could handle?"

"You couldn't have known," I said, trying to reassure her. "Before the stroke, Kelly would have been right in the middle of all the Rickenbaugh commotion. It's fine; don't worry. Let's just try to do it differently from now on."

As we limited her visitors and brought calm to her room, Kelly began to seem less agitated during the day and sleep better through the night. We knew that sleep was of the utmost importance for the brain to heal, so this seemed to be another step in the right direction.

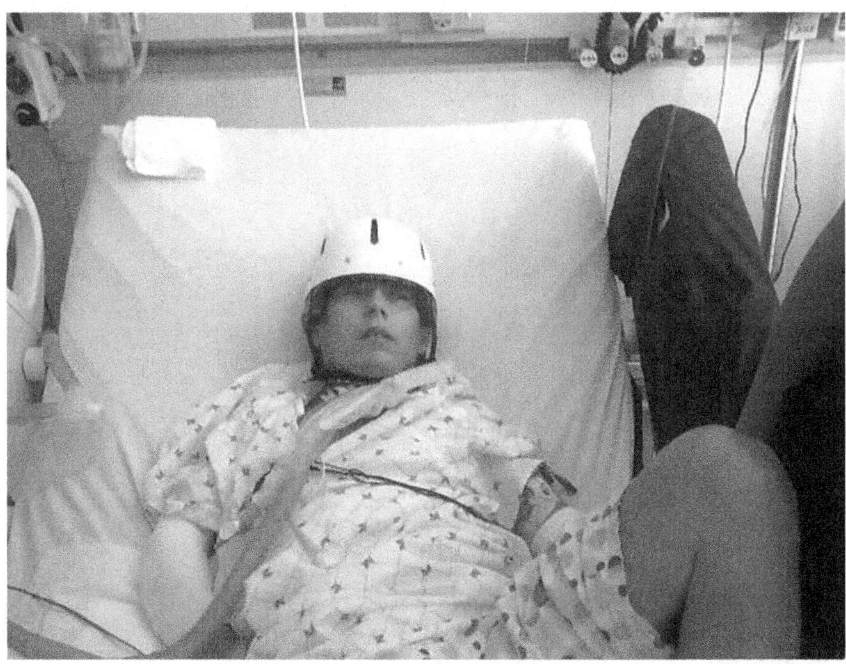

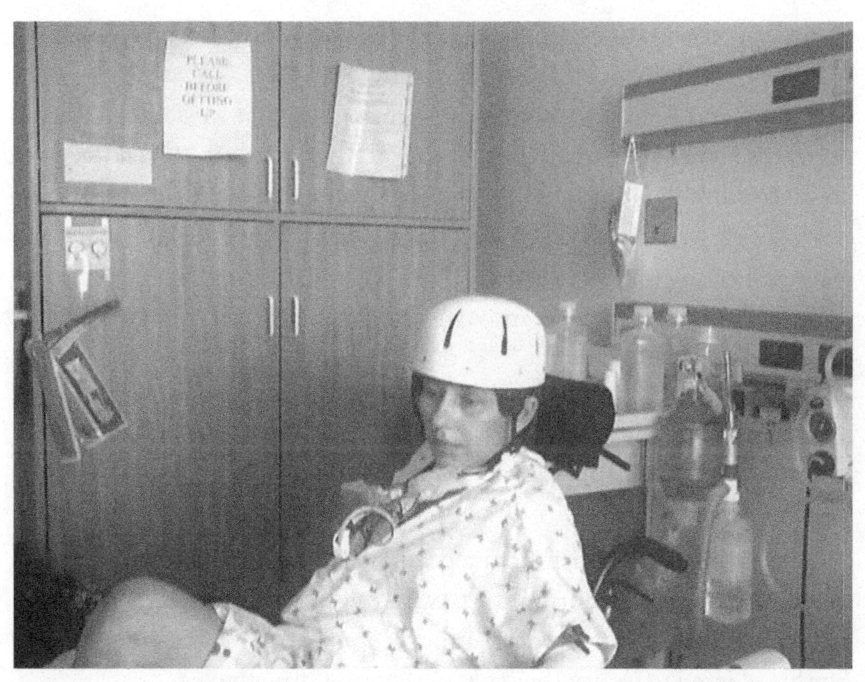

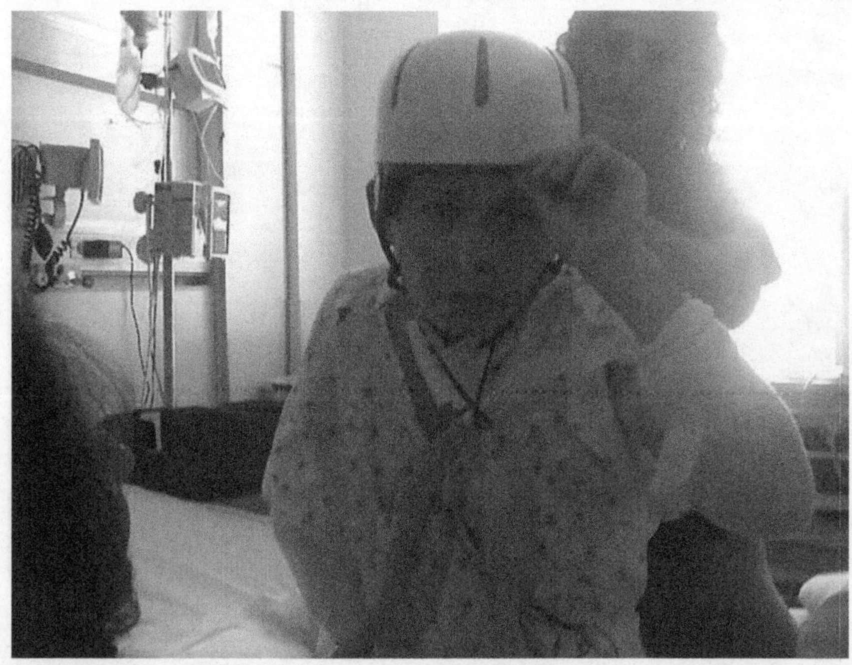

Amazing Progress

Before I returned from Minneapolis, they had Kelly up and walking in therapy. The progress felt so fast to me; as Kathie reported this development to me over the phone, I couldn't believe they had her up trying to walk on the bars. Only days earlier, she had arrived still on the ventilator and semiconscious.

By September 17, when I was due to return home, Kelly was walking, with assistance, the whole length of her hall. She'd learned to write her name left-handed. When a friend stopped by after her nursing shift and challenged Kelly to a friendly game of tic-tac-toe, Kelly loved it—and she loved winning even more.

After a good performance on a swallow test, Kelly graduated to nectar liquids and soft, mushy foods the consistency of cat food. Katie remarked, "I know she is not herself yet, because she is actually eating these foods!"

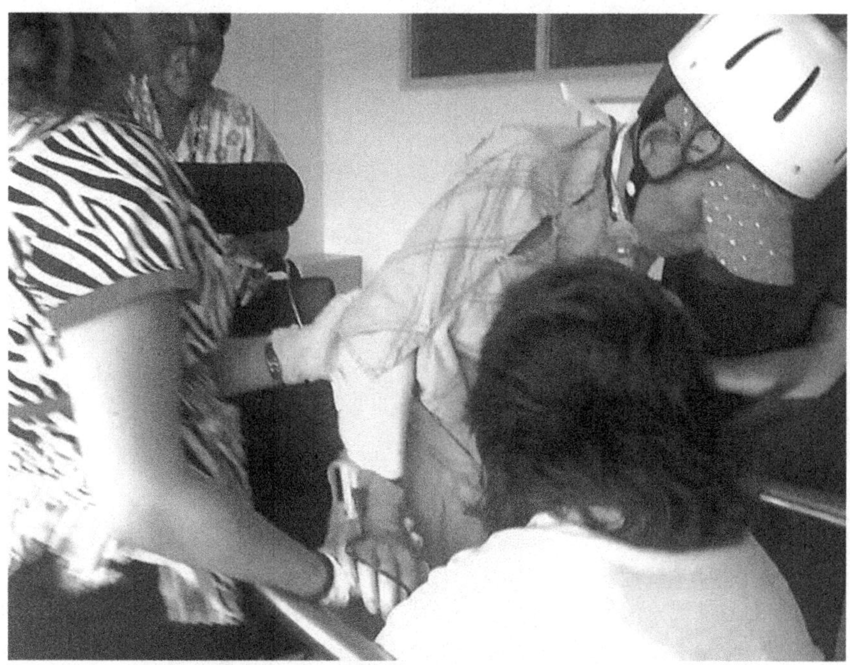

Finally, just before I came home, Kelly was able to have the trachea plug inserted, which dramatically helped her regain her speech.

"Brad, she is really making up for lost time with a lot of talking," Katie told me. "You wouldn't believe it! Everyone says she's just phenomenal! She works so hard to try to find the words. She even gave me and Rob a hard time about where we have been and said we should be there more! Her voice sounds a little different, but it's her, Brad! She's still Kelly!" This post from the CarePages captured her progress well for our social network of support. Posts like these were great to keep friends, family, and colleagues up to date on her progress, and she appreciated them even more when she was able to read them months later.

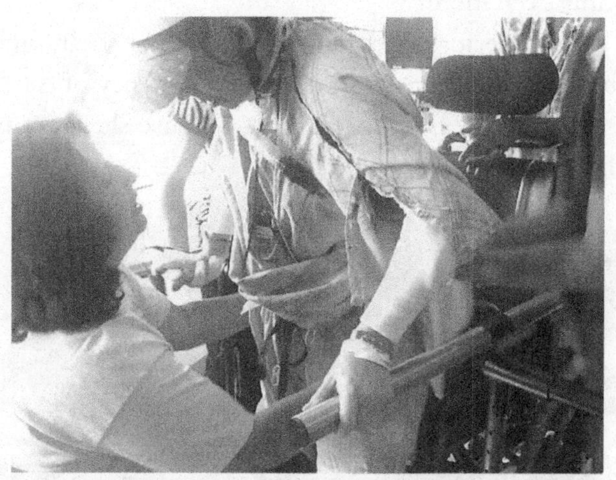

September 16, 2009, 7:10 p.m.
Rehab Continues!

Kelly had another exciting and very busy day at rehab today, filled with lots of physical therapy and speech/language therapy. She was very responsive to all therapy, and we are hoping that the trachea plug will be put in sooner rather than later to help with her communication, although we are all enjoying the faces she is making at us to try to communicate her thoughts and emotions to certain people and therapies.

She is trying to mouth words but gets overstimulated and has to take a break sometimes. The physical therapist worked with her on sitting in the specialized chair and standing using parallel bars. She was very excited to see her Anna Banana and teared up while Anna was talking to her. She was most excited today to know that Brad was coming in the evening straight from the airport. She mouthed several times that she could not wait to see him and would smile ear to ear when you reminded her that he was on his way. She is making tons of progress but still needs her rest to let her brain rejuvenate.

We can't wait to see what new things tomorrow brings!

LYMI,

Team Kelly

After getting the updates while I was on the road, to say that I was less than focused in my work meetings would be an understatement. Hearing the news of Kelly's amazing progress in my absence was both exhilarating and bittersweet. I couldn't believe I had missed all these milestones, and I was anxious to get back home to see her and hear her voice again.

During those early days, I spent a lot of time hoping and praying that Kelly would recover, but at that point, I didn't even really know what recovery would mean for her. I was operating day to day, looking for small improvements and steady progress, without thinking too much about the long-term implications of our situation.

We would cross each bridge when we came to it.

For now, she was breathing well on her own and recalling and saying new words each day. Her right leg was noticeably more mobile. She made a point to move it around, although she couldn't bend it on her own. Always up for a challenge, she seemed to love her therapists and doing therapy.

The short-term goal was for her to be released from the LTAC unit and move to a full rehab floor, where we could ramp up her therapy to a minimum of three hours a day on our way to the maximum of five hours. We were also working toward removing her stomach tube to make things more comfortable for her. The pace of her progress had astonished the rehab staff, and we fully expected it to continue or accelerate with more therapy.

One day, as we went through the cards that her many well-wishers had sent, Kelly indicated she wanted me to thank everyone. In her own way, she was trying to tell me that things were going to be okay.

She was our living proof that prayers work and miracles happen every day.

The Proposal

My personal experience during those early days showed me that anything you can do as the caregiver to spark memories or positive emotions for the survivor can be therapeutic. Importantly, this is true not only for the survivor but also for the caregiver and support network. There is nothing more important at this stage of recovery than positive and motivational reminders of past experiences and relationships.

Of course, every situation is different, but energized and excited by the news of Kelly's progress, I hatched a plan that would surprise anyone who knew me before the day that everything changed.

With our wedding anniversary approaching in late September, I decided that when I got back from my work trip, I would propose to Kelly again.

She had gone nearly three weeks without her wedding ring, which had been removed for the surgery. I didn't know if she realized she didn't have it. In fact, I didn't know for sure that she knew who I was or that we were married. All I knew was that she seemed to like having me around. It was a start.

Later that week, after I landed at the airport, I stopped at home to pick up the ring and headed for the rehab facility. I greeted Kathie and Rick with a hug before dismissing them from their posts as chief caregivers in my absence.

Kelly had improved a lot in the few days I had been gone. Even though her family had kept me up to speed, it still surprised and humbled me to witness her improvement in person. She smiled when she saw me.

We sat together for a while quietly, as I wanted to let her adjust to my presence at her own speed. The last thing I wanted was for her to get overstimulated before I could pop the question. I told her about my trip and conveyed how happy I'd been to hear about her progress, how proud of her I was, and how much I'd wanted to come home to her again.

When there was nothing left to tell, I took my gamble.

I got down on one knee next to her bed and pulled the ring from my pocket. To my surprise, my own heart was pounding as though this were the first time.

"Will you marry me?" I asked.

She stared at me. I couldn't tell if the look on her face was disbelief or misunderstanding.

"Will you marry me?" I repeated slowly. "Again?" I showed her the ring.

Tears filled her eyes. She nodded as enthusiastically as she could and mouthed the word *yes*.

As I put her ring back in its rightful place on her finger for the first time in weeks, I felt as if we might have a shot at coming back from this together.

That night, the most romantic restaurant had nothing on our hospital room. We sat comfortably together, and I thought about how far we had come in the week since leaving the ICU.

The next day, out of nowhere, she said, "You don't have a clue," and kicked me when I couldn't understand where she wanted me to put her oscillating fan.

"I guess you're getting back to your old self," I said, thrilled at this glimpse of the real Kelly. "You see, we really are husband and wife."

Concert in the Courtyard

Weather-wise, we were having one of the best autumns I can remember in Cincinnati. Kelly was getting better, but she was still not completely cognitively there. Still, I knew her well enough to know she would like to be outdoors. The weekend after our reengagement, her parents and I took her for her first outdoor field trip, a jazz concert in the courtyard at the rehab facility. We wheeled her out in her deluxe chair, and we got some soda at the little concession stand.

Despite how much uncharted territory we'd covered in the last few weeks and how far we still had to go, on that afternoon in the courtyard, with the lively jazz music in our ears and the sunny blue sky overhead, the first sense of a new normal started to take hold.

The revisited proposal wasn't just an entertaining gesture to lighten the mood. It wasn't just an effort to jog Kelly's memory and bring a little more of her old self out of the fog of her recovery. It was a renewal of our commitment to each other, to seeing this thing through. Whether on the plane home from vacation, by a hospital bed, or in a rehab facility courtyard, my place was at Kelly's side—always.

If We Only Knew: Inpatient Rehab Tips

- Things move fast. Unlike in the ICU, good things happen fast in rehab. Their goal is to get the patient out of rehab, and the only way out is independence or as close as the patient can get to independence in a matter of weeks.

- Get to know the staff. Just as in the ICU, getting to know the nurse's aides, nurses, doctors, and therapists is critical.

- Have patience. Communication, lack of memory, and cognitive and physical limitations are common for TBI victims. They will be frustrated, and so will you. In most cases, they are still figuring out what happened, so be patient, and be careful with tone of voice and stimulation levels. Less is more in the early days and weeks.

- Be prepared for aphasia. The inability to find and form words is common if the left side of the brain is damaged. Communication will be next to impossible even when the drugs start to wear off, and you'll need to pay close attention to what the patient (not you or anyone else) needs. Ask the doctors if they think aphasia will be a challenge for the patient, and develop a plan to assist.

- You will need a quarterback. The hospital staff will not coordinate, communicate, and organize everything for your loved one, and the first week is critical in terms of getting the lay of the land and understanding the daily regimen and goals. Document the names, specialties, and affiliations of the doctors and nurses. Keep a list of medications, test results, and any progress or therapies. Know when visiting hours are and when the doctors are expected to visit the patient so that you know when to be there to ask questions on behalf of the patient. You might have to be there all day and all night at first to ensure the patient is getting the right level of care with the right specialists, just as I had to do to ensure Kelly had a full-time aide at first. See appendix B for more information.

CHAPTER 5

What Happened to September?

Kelly

I wish I could clearly chronicle my thoughts and feelings and the events during this time or even distinguish which ones were real and which were imagined, but the truth is, I'm not completely sure. I must have been in and out of consciousness between the airport and the hospital, and I have only a few vague memories, such as looking up at the ceiling and realizing someone was wheeling me. I remember seeing double doors and feeling as if I were floating along. The white tiles of the ceiling rolled by, blurring together.

When I woke up again, I was surrounded by machines, and everything was white. I was obviously in a hospital. I saw buttons and heard beeping and whirring, but I felt no pain. *Am I dreaming?* I wondered. *I remember. I had something. Some kind of accident.* I drifted in and out, and every once in a while, I would open my eyes, see the same area, and think, *Okay, I'm still dreaming.* Then I'd fall back asleep.

I saw people, familiar but blurry faces. *They look worried. I feel okay, but obviously this was something more than just a headache.*

I wanted to just say, "I want this or that." I was frustrated, and I would think about it at night. *Okay, I'm going to talk. I'm going to talk about that tomorrow morning when somebody comes.* But when tomorrow came, I still couldn't get the words out.

It seems now as if I should have been frightened, but I just kept going back to sleep. Maybe I did that on purpose to get away from the worry.

Plus, I was just so tired. People would visit for what felt like ten hours, and I couldn't tell them to go away. *Just go away and leave me alone,* I thought, but no words came.

I didn't exactly recognize my parents, but I did recognize their voices. They would say my name, so I knew that obviously, I was Kelly. My dad wasn't talking a lot, and I knew, somehow, that wasn't normal. I could tell he was frightened, which confirmed for me that this situation was serious.

Then there was another person, a nice woman who tried to get me up out of the bed. I was not happy with that at all.

"I don't want to do this. Stop it!" I tried to tell her, but she didn't seem to understand. She wanted to get me up, to walk me around. There were chairs and straps and all types of apparatuses. "My head hurts. I can't do it," I tried to tell her, but no words came out.

I wanted to rattle people and say, "What's going on?" I've always been independent, and I was quickly learning how to cope with the opposite, which was frustrating. I just wanted to get out of that bed on my own and walk out of there, but when I tried to move my right arm and leg, nothing happened.

There were all these people—so many people in one little area. It was overwhelming. They talked and talked, all at once. Sometimes they talked to me, and it seemed as if they were shouting. Sometimes they ignored me completely and just shouted at each other. Everything blurred together.

Despite all that talking, nobody told me anything about what had happened or what was going on.

I have always talked to God, morning and night, about my day and what I can do to help other people. I knew he didn't need words, so when I couldn't talk to the world around me, I talked to him in my mind.

I remember vividly the first great moment, which was a Bengals game that my family and I watched together on the small TV in my room. My dad had bought me a Bengals scarf, and as he wrapped it around my neck, I realized, *I think I like this.* I didn't remember watching football or wearing Bengals gear, but the experience felt familiar and normal, and I wasn't thinking about all my new challenges and fears. *Okay, that's something. This is something that we do.* I remember that my dad was happy, so I was happy.

Hi. Have We Met?

I knew that this guy Brad was coming around. I kind of thought that we were something, that there was something between us. When I saw him, I would think, *Oh, that's Brad,* but it didn't occur to me that we were married.

I only knew that this guy was uplifting—not too happy but not too sad, just in between. He would talk to me, but he wouldn't talk too loudly or too quietly. He was just an even-keeled person I could sit with. He would hold my hand. It was comforting.

Everything was so loud. It was too much for people to approach me too quickly. My family is boisterous. If somebody stops talking and doesn't finish a sentence, someone else just jumps in, and it gets louder and louder. It was too much for me, and I tried to communicate that.

I don't want to see that. I don't want to hear it. No, no, no, no, no, no, no. I'm not ready. I'm not ready. I'm not ready.

As I became more lucid, I began to figure out ways to communicate even though I couldn't speak. I needed to smile to indicate that something was good or frown if something was bad. I couldn't smile properly, but I would make some kind of movement of my mouth, almost like a grimace, and people always said, "Oh, look, she's smiling."

My mom was really good because she could talk or not talk. I would bang on the table if I needed something, and she would figure it out.

I got used to having my mom, my dad, and that other guy, Brad, with me every day. Other people came in and out, and I'd think, *Who are these people?* Then, suddenly, one day Brad wasn't there.

The break in routine scared me. I remember that I wanted him back. I needed him back. I was unhappy, which my mom picked up on, and she said, "Oh, he can't come today, but he's going to be here tomorrow."

I smiled, while inside I thought, *Okay, you should have told me that.*

As promised, Brad did finally come back. There was a candle on the table next to my bed—a fake, battery-operated candle that my mom had brought. Brad and I were talking. Well, I was doing more listening than talking, but in any case, I knew I liked him.

That day, I was sitting in my chair, and he said, "Something, something, something, something, something."

Then there was a ring—a really nice ring. He bent down on one knee and repeated himself, and I figured out that he was asking me a question.

He was just so cute and nice, and he was there with me again, so I said yes. Or I said, "Ss."

It wasn't loud, because it was still hard and a little painful to talk. But it was nice, and I didn't cry. Then we ate French toast for dinner. He seemed happy, and I felt happy. It started to come together for me: *Either we're already engaged, or we're married.*

The day I went outside for the jazz concert in the courtyard, I felt the happiest I'd ever been. They brought me new outfits from home and finally got me out of those four walls. Again, I didn't exactly remember being at concerts or what they were, but somehow I knew that I liked music and how it made me feel.

It's perfect. Even though it's not perfect, it's perfect. I'm outside. My parents are here. And Brad.

If We Only Knew: Welcome Back

- Pictures and names are helpful. Memory will likely be affected, so bring pictures of family and friends for the room, and go over them with the patient to try to help him or her re-create familiarity and know who is visiting. Importantly, the patient might not know you, so prepare yourself and help him or her.

- Remember, the patient might be experiencing complex inabilities that can seem frustrating. Kelly knew what she wanted to do and say but couldn't do or say it at first. Don't take any expressions of frustration personally.

- Rest is essential. When the patient is between therapy and tests, rest is the most important thing for the brain to heal and the person to recover for the next day's activities. Just like after a workout, your muscles need to rest. The same goes for the brain.

- Overstimulation is counterproductive. As much as everyone wants to maximize visiting hours to show support, what the patient needs is carefully controlled visitation and one or two people max talking and interacting. This is especially true if the patient was asleep for several weeks, as Kelly was.

CHAPTER 6

Only Six Months?

Brad

Throughout our stay in long-term acute care, the rehab staff shared a piece of common wisdom in stroke treatment: "Studies have shown that most motor and sensory recovery is finished by the six-month mark."

At first, this terrified us. *Six months? Only six months?* She could barely speak, she couldn't remember our names, and it had already been almost a month. *How much better can she possibly get in just six months?*

But as she continued to defy expectations and impress everyone with her exponential progress, we chose to embrace the six-month deadline. It became our mantra and our motivation.

Reflecting back, we can see that the six-month time frame symbolizes a more interesting insight for anyone going through traumatic brain injury recovery. There is much that is unknown about the brain. It is fascinating and alarming all at once. The questions on people's minds are the same, whether or not they say them out loud. How much can their loved ones recover? Will they be able to walk, talk, read, write, and take care of themselves? Will they remember their lives and dreams or have other cognitive limitations? How will they adjust, and how will they be able to cope? It's okay and natural to ask, but when the doctors tell you, "It's too early to tell," or say they can't speculate, it's the truth. Every case is different, and the situation largely depends on the damage and, most importantly, the effort and motivation of the survivor and his or her support network.

Medical specialists will cite precedent and popular thinking when answering questions about recovery. Some doctors will say the bulk of improvement is limited to three months, and some will say six months or a year, but in reality, you can improve forever, both physically and cognitively. The biggest gains are typically made early on, but the brain and its neural possibilities are beyond the scope of textbooks and clinical trials. The truth is that even if there is damage, the brain has the ability to find new pathways to accomplish a task. The process might not be as fast or as graceful, but it can be functional. There will be some things that survivors can no longer do or not do at the level they used to, but they won't know if they don't try, and the patients' will to get better is infectious for therapists and staff. Don't limit the expectations of you or your family member to those of the doctors; instead, set your own goals together. The small wins are huge for a patient early on. They all add up over time.

Just as in the ICU, Kelly's personality and energy, as well as good food and drink, won over the staff. Two weeks into rehab, we finally got word that Kelly was ready to be moved to the full-time rehab floor. Knowing this was an important step, Susan and Kelly's other girlfriend aides helped pack her stuff up and bid her a teary farewell.

"Six months, Kelly," I told her as we settled into her new ground-floor room and prepared for intensive rehab.

Time to Step It Up

Kelly settled into her new room. It was the first private room she'd had since the journey began, which made all of Team Kelly happy. She jumped into the longer hours of therapy and began to win over the staff on her new floor, just as she had charmed the staffs at her previous stops.

Rehabilitation was a full-time job, an eight-hour workday that began at six thirty in the morning. As with the first day of school, we had new therapists, doctors, nurses, and aides to meet.

My company was going through a tough year, the upside of which was that my travel was limited, and I could do most of my work via e-mail and phone calls, so I set up shop in the rehab facility. I showed up every morning by ten or eleven, after Kelly's morning bathing and medication routine. I'd join the therapy and stay until ten or eleven at night, working in my cafeteria "office" when Kelly was resting between therapy sessions. We ate most meals together in her room. The facility brought me food as well. The staff began to know me by name and would say hello and good-bye when they changed shifts in the morning and evening.

It was an exhausting time, but adrenaline kept me going.

Kelly enjoyed going through all the get-well cards and reading all the kind messages from her family and friends on her CarePages. She was still easily overstimulated and frustrated by a constant flow of different visitors, so we limited the visits from immediate family members to only one or two people per day. Right away, we saw her frustration level decrease, and her more positive attitude began to return.

When the brain and body are healing and getting stronger, nothing is more important than rest. She needed to recover in the afternoons and needed time alone to do that. We policed that time carefully once we understood its importance.

Kelly was able to walk short distances with some assistance, and she had a wheelchair in her room to get from the bed to the bathroom and to her rehab sessions. The staff helped her shower and take care of her other personal needs, since she only had the use of one arm and leg.

Of all these obstacles, communication with Kelly was the most frustrating, limited to hand signals and trial-and-error guessing of what she needed or wanted. She would shake her head and point angrily, not understanding how it wasn't crystal clear what she required. The speech and occupational therapists gave us some laminated cards with pictures of faces ranging from a smile to a frown and a pain scale. Other cards showed common items, such as food, drink, a toilet, TV, lights, and medicine. These cards helped us communicate when she couldn't speak or move both of her hands, and they started to jog her memory on the names of things. It was a start.

I couldn't imagine how difficult it had to be for her. In fact, I tried not to imagine it in her presence, because it would break me down to see her that way. She needed strength and encouragement from me, not signs of weakness. As tough as it was for me mentally and emotionally, whenever I started to feel sorry for myself, my thoughts immediately returned to Kelly. What I was feeling was nothing compared to what she was going through. The hard work was just beginning.

Control

Kelly was young and fit, so from a physical standpoint, even from the beginning, we could see big progress every day. I could see that she might have some long-term physical challenges, but those seemed manageable to me.

More alarming to me were the cognitive and speech issues. In the first speech session, she played the game Uno with a couple of other patients. The experience was beyond comprehension and words for me as I watched her struggle to match the colors or numbers or to follow the purpose of the game. It was Uno—how could this be her?

She knew it wasn't going well and at first just stared at the cards and the therapist, trying to guess correctly, but she didn't give up, and over the course of the session, I could see her improve. I didn't realize it then, but in just that one-hour session, her brain rebuilt pathways to give her the answers.

In another session, they had her match pictures with the names of objects. The therapist would point to a figure on a card, such as a dog, cat, or bird, and say, "What's that?" She'd say, "I don't know. Control."

Kelly had what is called aphasia, which is the inability to originate and form words to speak. It is fairly common if the stroke affected the communication centers in the brain. In Kelly's case, she had acute aphasia early on, so she would form and say the word in her brain, but what came out was a different word or word fragment. It's common for aphasia patients to substitute a different word when they can't produce the correct one. (I remember reading that Gabby Giffords's husband said the word she gravitated toward was *chicken*.) Kelly used the word *control* and the phrase "going to be okay." Those were her go-to words when she was having trouble finding the right ones, so she said them for nearly everything, which made verbal communication next to impossible.

I think she realized at that point that her speech was not right. She knew what she was trying to say, and it sounded right in her mind, but when it came out, it was something totally different. She didn't comprehend why I couldn't understand her, because the words sounded right to her. She would get frustrated, and pretty quickly, she did not want me attending her speech therapy sessions.

The rehab staff didn't set expectations for me, because they really didn't know how her brain would respond. The "You have six months" warning rang in my head, taunting me. It seemed she had lost all of her language ability, an ability that had taken years of her life to develop. I wondered how much progress she could possibly make in the next five months.

There was nothing to do but try to hide my emotions and be supportive. I tried like hell not to get frustrated, because I knew that would only make the situation worse. I didn't want her to know how scared I was or how much I worried that her speech wouldn't improve.

Mostly, I was figuring out on my own how to mentally deal with all the unknowns and accept that I had no control of the situation. I talked to some of her therapists who had dealt with family members, and they all suggested I seek some sort of support. There were caregiver support groups at the rehab center, and I don't remember now why I didn't join any of those. I think it was just a conflict with my schedule, and Kelly was so young that I couldn't imagine anyone with common challenges. There was too much to do, and she needed me there with her. In hindsight, I should have at least gone to see if it would be informative or helpful. I now know there were likely plenty of other younger couples or families there going through the same process. Instead, I just stayed on top of the therapists for tips and advice.

The Lightbulb Moment

Even with the language barrier, I could see Kelly's personality returning.

One day I went into the restroom with her. She pulled her wheelchair up to the sink to wash her hands. As I watched, she reached over with her left hand, picked her right arm up, placed it in the sink, and proceeded to wash her hands. I fought back tears while watching her deal in such a matter-of-fact way with her new reality.

That memory will stick with me for the rest of my life. Kelly was always determined, and it looked like that wasn't going to change. She was clearly coming to grips with all that was going on with her body, even if I wasn't.

Not that she never complained. She did—at me, to me, to the doctors, to the nurses. But it wasn't complaining so much as insisting that things be a certain way. In her room, she had her own chest of drawers, and we decorated it with photographs and knickknacks from home. We brought her clothes for sleeping and for her daytime activities. She wanted them folded just so and organized in a certain way in her drawers.

On Friday, September 25, Kelly experienced a major breakthrough. The speech therapist, Theresa, left a monthly calendar on the bulletin board. After lunch and much discussion, I realized Kelly was asking about the calendar.

"Today is September 25," I said.

She looked at me, clearly puzzled.

"Do you remember what happened at the airport?" I asked.

"Yes," Kelly replied, but I could tell she was still confused, and I wasn't sure if she really understood the question.

"You have been very sick," I explained. "You're on medication, and you've been sleeping since August 30." I pointed to the date on the calendar.

She was in disbelief that she had been asleep for that long and, as she would later say, "lost that time." We flipped the calendar back and forth, and I showed her the CarePages entries that chronicled the days.

Suddenly, she got it. It was as if a lightbulb went off in her head, and I could tell it all made sense to her at that moment. Where the time had gone, why she was confused—it all fell into place. Tears welled in her eyes, but she seemed relieved to finally understand to some degree what had happened, even if she couldn't piece together all the details just yet.

Later, she told me she thought it was a few hours or a day that she had been unconscious, but she had no recollection of the airport or the EMTs.

Once she gained some realization of her situation and how much time had passed, her single focus became going home. Channeling her energy toward a focused goal is something that Kelly has always done, and she realized that the way to get home was to do everything her therapists asked of her and then some. So that became her job—to get better and recover everything she could. I still didn't know if she fully understood what had happened, but she was focused on her recovery.

Her growing sense of the passage of time and what had happened was an important first step on her road to reclaiming her life. I was happy for her realization, but it pained me to think about what must have been running through her mind when she was alone at night with her thoughts and fears. I wished I could help her through that, but how could I? It was all on her to figure it out in that quiet, dark, lonely hospital room. She didn't deserve this. Things had to get better for her.

Kelly

When we moved downstairs to the full rehab floor, I was really still out of it, trying to figure out where I was, what had happened, and who everyone was that I was supposed to know. I felt as if I were watching things happen from outside of my body at times. It probably didn't help that I was still taking a cocktail of seizure and pain meds that would have slowed down a grown man. Still, that wasn't going to slow me down in therapy. I liked being out of the bed and doing things.

I was happy to have my own room. There was an interesting piece of art on the wall; it was round, and it had numbers around the outside of the circle and pointers that moved around the circle. I didn't realize at the time that it was a clock.

Someone had pasted pictures of family members on the wall, with their names written on Post-its underneath their pictures. My family thought that would help me recognize people when they came to visit. The funny thing was, I couldn't read the names, but my family didn't know that. I would think, *Okay, so somebody needs to tell me what this person's name is, because I can't read that.* When visitors arrived, I would focus on their faces and say to Brad or my mom, "What's their name? What's their name? Name, name, name?" I'd guess, "Kelly? Wait. No, it's not me." Then I'd say, "Katie?" I worked hard on putting names with faces and then remembering them from visit to visit.

I was doing therapy for three to five hours a day. Physical therapy was the easiest for me. It involved walking and trying to grip and lift my arm and leg. I liked the challenge of learning to walk again and building up my strength, and I could see progress almost every day.

I had no vision in my right eye for a while and couldn't feel or see my right leg and arm, so I had no awareness that they were there. For example, I would eat everything I could see on my plate, and then someone would turn the plate around, and half the food was still there. Now I know that is called right-side neglect. This is a common condition for stroke victims, because there is a lack of sensation and feeling on the side of the body affected by the stroke—so you don't even realize it's there. It is the side of the body opposite the brain hemisphere the stroke occurred in (e.g., a stroke in the left side of brain will result in weakness of the right side of the body). My right-side neglect was worse because of my vision limitations.

A big part of my therapy was learning to be aware of my right side, even though it didn't function yet at that point. I could trap my arm or hand in my chair or bed or run over my leg or foot with my wheelchair if I wasn't careful. I wore a sling or strap to protect my arm from just hanging and to get muscle tone back.

The occupational therapy team was focused on exercises related to activities and function of my upper body. They developed goals for me so that I could take care of myself with regard to basic day-to-day activities, such as bathing, dressing, and eating. They gave me exercises related to improving my visual and spatial impairments, for safety and increased independence. The occupational therapists were young and full of energy, so I felt as if I needed to keep up. It was great for me to have goals that I could work toward.

I also had speech therapy every day for an hour or so. We did sessions with other patients, usually a fun activity, such as cards. The group included mostly older people and me. We played with Uno cards, trying to name the colors. The therapist would ask, "What's that color?" and I'd say, "No?"

I was pretty smart before my stroke. I had a job that relied on words, writing, and speaking. I had been on the television news as a spokesperson for the college where I was employed. So being unable to name a dog or a chair made me feel dumb, like a baby. Sometimes I'd get frustrated and depressed about it, and there were moments when I thought about giving up.

What's going on? I found myself asking yet again.

Like a Nightmare

I had a short span of solitary time after the end of the workday until my evening medicine would knock me out. I used this time to reflect and try to reassure myself about what was coming next. I would plan what I would magically be able to say the next morning. I was confident that the next morning, I would be able to talk.

But then the next morning would come, my mouth would move, and sound would come out, but no one could understand me. It was like a nightmare. I was terrified that I would never learn to talk again.

Nights were by far the hardest and loneliest time. Every night, the aide would give me my evening medicine and then lock the bottle in a cabinet before she shackled me to the bed.

More than once, I found myself thinking, *Gosh, if I could only get to that medicine cabinet. I could take some more pills and go to sleep—just go to sleep forever, and this would be over. That would be so easy. And that would be fine with me.*

Then I'd look down at the restraints keeping me bound to the bed, and I'd remember that I couldn't even move that well without help. Even if I really wanted to get to the cabinet, I was alone, dependent, and helpless.

Still, the absurdity of the situation wasn't lost on me, and I could even laugh about it in my head in a sarcastic, cynical way.

Okay, I must be getting better, because I'm laughing and planning and thinking about all those things that I just like to think about.

I'm not just a drone. I'm still me.

I'm Here—Talk to Me

I've always preferred structure in my life, and now it was more critical than ever. I needed a set schedule with explicit goals that I could work toward and mark my progress against.

I don't remember the speech therapist's calendar on the wall or Brad walking me through the timeline of my hospitalization. What I do remember is saying to my mom, "I want to check the day off every day. I think regular people check every day off."

She brought me a calendar and opened it to the current date.

"Mom, why does the calendar say it's September?" I asked her. I thought it was still August.

"It is September. Late September. You've been sleeping for most of this month," she explained.

That freaked me out. Suddenly, more than a month was missing. The time was just gone—lost. I was devastated.

During the whole month of September, nobody had told me anything. The doctors, surgeons, and nurses would talk to Brad or my mom but not to me.

In the beginning, they weren't sure how much I could take in, I suppose, and for a while, I couldn't understand much anyway. Everything sounded like gibberish.

Then, when I was better able to understand, people didn't want to stress me out with too much detail about what had occurred. They were looking out for what they thought was my best interest, but I was frustrated at being treated as if I were invisible or, worse, stupid. I said several times to Brad, "I'm here—talk to me."

Finally, they told me that I had suffered a stroke, but that wasn't much help. Like most people, I had read about cancer and heart disease, but I didn't really even know what stroke was. I can't really even offer any suggestions here other than to tell the caregivers that the patients (like me) probably can't process that level of detail, because they are still heavily medicated, and their brains are still healing from the trauma. You could maybe try to explain in simpler terms, but I'm not sure it's helpful, because I didn't even realize yet that I had been asleep for two weeks. Providing too much information could also backfire if the patients are knowledgeable about stroke and get depressed about what has happened, when they need to be getting up and moving.

All I knew then was that in order to recover and go home, I had to meet my goals in therapy, so I decided to work harder every day.

No one had ever told me that half of my skull had been removed either. I knew I wore a helmet when I was out of the bed and a ball cap when I was in bed, but I didn't know why, and I didn't think too much about it. They ultimately informed me that I needed to have the missing piece of my skull replaced before I could go home. That meant surgery.

It's hard for me to describe my emotions and thoughts before the surgery to reattach my skull. I don't even know that I acknowledged what was going to happen. I had no concept of time or any idea why my brain and body weren't working.

Brad and my family told me that having surgery was a big next step for me to get better, and they were excited for me, so I had to trust that they were helping. I knew the situation was serious, but I also knew I didn't have a choice if I wanted to get better. Not knowing what was happening, combined with my medicine, kept me from worrying too much.

At that stage, the surgery was just another set of doctors around me, doing things that I hoped were going to help.

Brad

It's hard to imagine you can look forward to brain surgery, but that's what we were doing. Kelly's surgery to replace the piece of her skull that had been removed was another step along her road to recovery, so we were anxious to take that step. It would also mean that she could lose the helmet, and we were sure she'd be happy about that.

The morning of the surgery, Kelly would be transferred by ambulance from the rehab facility back to the university hospital, where the missing piece of her skull had been kept frozen in storage.

"Do I travel in the ambulance with her?" I asked.

"No, she'll be fine. Everything is taken care of," one of her nurses assured me.

But when I arrived at the hospital at seven thirty in the morning on the day of surgery, I discovered Kelly wearing a tag that said, "Jane Doe."

I was flabbergasted at this. I had been told her file would go with her, yet there we were, and they didn't even know who she was.

Just then, the anesthesiologist for her surgery entered the room. The first question out of his mouth to Kelly was "Are you allergic to anything?"

She said, "No," which, in Kelly-speak, meant yes.

I jumped in. "Yes, she is. She's allergic to penicillin. She's got aphasia—she can't talk, and if she does talk, she might say the opposite of what she means. It's all right there in the file."

Her entire medical record was sitting at the end of her bed, but it seemed that no one had read it. *What if they had given her penicillin? Would they even have figured out who she was? How in the world could this have happened?*

While her doctors were all great, and we owed them her life, the record-keeping-handoff process and communication in health care seemed broken to me. I tried not to imagine what could have happened had I not been there.

Once we had her identity and allergy issues straightened out and I was convinced that they knew what they were doing, they wheeled Kelly off to the operating room. Kelly's parents and sister kept vigil with me for the three-hour operation.

Kathie and Aunt Lorie went to the deli for some coffee, Rick settled into the waiting room to read the paper, and I went off to find a Wi-Fi hot spot to take a business call. It might seem odd to some that I could work at such a time, but sitting in the waiting room and watching the board change symbols was not exactly a productive experience. I knew Kelly would understand.

Twenty minutes later, I heard an emergency page over the loudspeaker. "Brad Marsh, please return to the OR waiting room."

I raced back to the waiting room in a near panic. This was much too soon for the surgery to be over. What in the world had gone wrong?

"They said the doctor wants to meet us ASAP," Kelly's dad told me, trying to keep his voice from shaking.

Shortly, the surgeon emerged, calming us immediately. "Don't worry," he said. "The surgery has not even begun. I just wanted to remind you that if we cannot get her skull to fit well enough, we will have to use a synthetic plate. It's better to have her own bone, but if we can't, it's the next-best option."

Relief overcame panic. I agreed, and it occurred to me to remind him to shave her entire head, not just the left side. Kelly wanted her hair, or lack of hair, to be all the same. He smiled as if to say, "Really?" and then agreed.

So we settled in to wait again, and the surgery was finally over by midafternoon. They had successfully replaced Kelly's own bone.

However, as luck would have it, we found ourselves trapped in the health care Bermuda Triangle called Friday. No one had thought to file the paperwork for Kelly's transfer back to rehab until too late in the day, so she would be spending the weekend in the hospital. I was sure she would be unhappy when I told her she would miss a day of rehab, but we were grateful to have cleared another hurdle and have another big step out of the way with her skull back in its rightful place.

After the morning identity mix-up and the red tape of transferring, my faith in the hospital process had been shaken, so I stayed at the hospital that night. I was a little worried about the pinhole drain and fifty-plus staples she still had in her head, but the doctor said the drain was a precaution and would close on its own. The staples looked painful to me, but Kelly didn't seem to mind.

In fact, Kelly looked so happy and cheerful that we dared to believe what many people had told us: healing would accelerate and memory would return quickly once her skull was put back in place.

No matter what, at least she didn't have to wear the helmet anymore, and we could finally start planning her departure from rehab and her return home.

Kelly

I woke up the morning after surgery and immediately needed to use the restroom. Two young women got me up out of bed, and I walked around a bit, testing out my movements, and then shuffled into the bathroom to take care of business.

As the aides helped me to the sink, I glanced up and saw someone, something, in the mirror.

Is that me?

The restrooms at the rehab facility did not have mirrors, so this was the first time I had seen myself since we'd left New Orleans on August 30.

No one had prepared me for what I saw there. My head was uncovered, with no bandages. My hair had been shaved, and a greenish antiseptic wash covered my forehead and neck. Large black staples punctuated the skin on my head, giving me a definitive Frankenstein look.

I didn't recognize myself and immediately broke down in tears. Until then, I hadn't known that I didn't have any hair. For the longest time, I'd just thought they had a ball cap on me and hadn't really thought much of it. The reality was devastating.

"Oh, Mom. Oh, Mom" was all I could say.

Even in my agitated state, I felt a little bit sorry for the two ladies who'd led me in there. Just as I had been unprepared for my own reflection, they didn't know they were about to face a meltdown. I made my way back to the bed, and they gave me a sedative to calm me down and put me back to sleep.

When I next woke up, a doctor was talking to two other guys who looked about twelve years old, like Doogie Howser. The doctor wasn't talking to me; he was talking to the two Doogies. Trying to get their attention, I said, "Hi," but they didn't seem interested in explaining anything to me. Instead, they fiddled with my neck a little bit and then got busy on their BlackBerrys.

All of a sudden, I heard a whoosh of air and felt as if I were suffocating. I could see that my mom was upset, and I was struggling and panting. The Doogies stood over me, just looking on.

I didn't realize that they had just removed my tracheotomy tube.

One of the Doogies slapped a gauze pad over the hole in my neck and said, "It's nothing to worry about. For a day or two, there will be some air escaping from this hole when she speaks, but it will subside fairly quickly."

How about a little preparation? I thought to myself.

This was the straw that broke the camel's back. When lunch arrived, it was not to my liking. This was something I could do something about. I picked up the hospital hamburger and heaved it across the room onto the floor. My mom looked at me in surprise but said nothing as she cleaned it up off the floor.

Moms understand. I had had it.

Later that afternoon, Brad brought me a real burger, not from the cafeteria. I don't eat much meat anymore, but something about having food from outside the hospital was comforting, and I ate the whole thing, along with the fries. It was my sweet, salty revenge on the unhelpful Doogies.

I made it through the rest of the weekend, and I never had been so happy to see someplace as I was when I checked back in to the rehab center on Monday. Now we were in the home stretch. It was time for moving on and really working toward my return home.

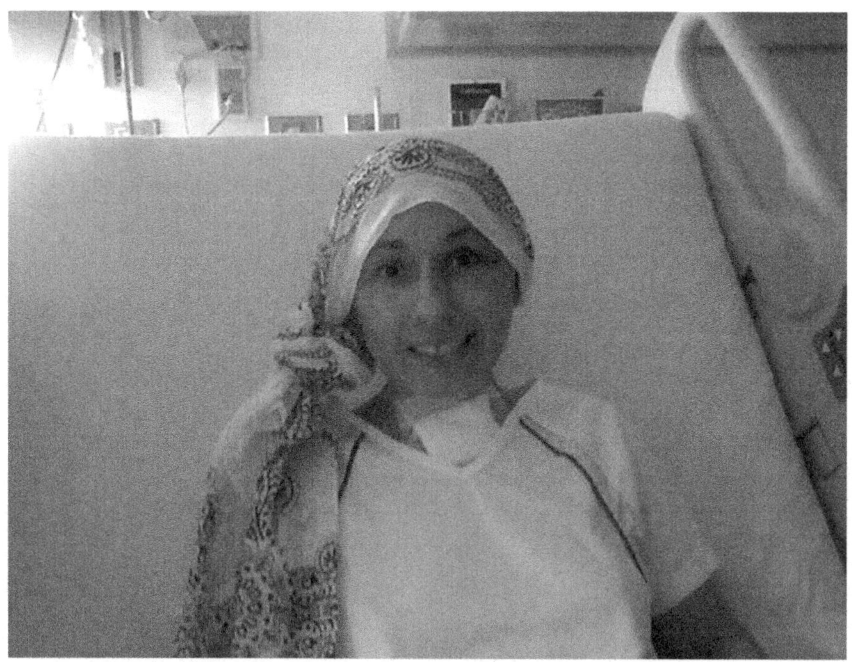

If We Only Knew: Therapy and Surgery Insights

- Don't panic. Watching your loved one struggle and fail to do basic things is terrifying, but the brain relearns skills faster than it learned them the first time. An ability can come back quickly once a new pathway is found, but it takes trial and error.

- Be an active participant. Teaching the brain to relearn things requires repetition, and the therapists only set the table. It's up to the patient and his or her caregiver to practice and do homework to improve. Plus, at some point, you will be home and have to lead the activities if you want your loved one to improve.

- Focus, and work. Most insurance will limit the time you have in inpatient, so take advantage of the focused care, and get as much out of it as you can. Finding a source of motivation for your survivor is critical, and everyone is different. For Kelly, it was the thought of getting home.

- There is a procedure for getting outpatient therapy to continue. Be sure you know what your insurance company requires, and keep records.

- Be present during surgery prep. You might not have to deal with any surgery, but if you do and your loved one cannot speak, someone needs to be there for the prep to ensure the routine questions the surgery staff asks are answered. Also plan to be with the patient when he or she wakes up.

- Rest. Rest is still the most important thing for improvement, even at this stage.

- Remember that improvement is infinite. You might have limited time in the rehab facility, but your brain will never stop improving.

CHAPTER 7

Did We Get Everything on the List?

Brad

The hard push for home began the day we returned to rehab. The therapists established explicit goals that Kelly would have to reach before being discharged.

She had to be able to dress herself and manage other independent living needs. She needed to be able to walk the length of the hallway while scanning the floor for cones. She would have to read, write, and express herself verbally in a basic way.

While Kelly was busy working toward her goals, Kathie and I had goals of our own. We would be the ones responsible for helping Kelly when she came home, and we needed to learn the skills necessary for that.

For instance, the therapists taught us the methods and techniques to help her walk with an assistance harness (strap), including up and down stairs, which has a specific technique: lead with the good foot up, and lead with the weak foot down. We had to be in front of her on the way down and behind her on the way up in case she lost balance. They showed us how to get her in and out of bed, the car, and chairs, using her wheelchair for stability. We of course always had to be conscious of her right arm and leg, which she could not feel and didn't know were there without a reminder. They showed us how Kelly should use her cane when she was ready and how to help her shower, stretch her muscles, and get her up off the floor if she fell. Of course, she also had to learn these techniques in case we weren't around, but until she was stronger, she was going to need our help for most everything.

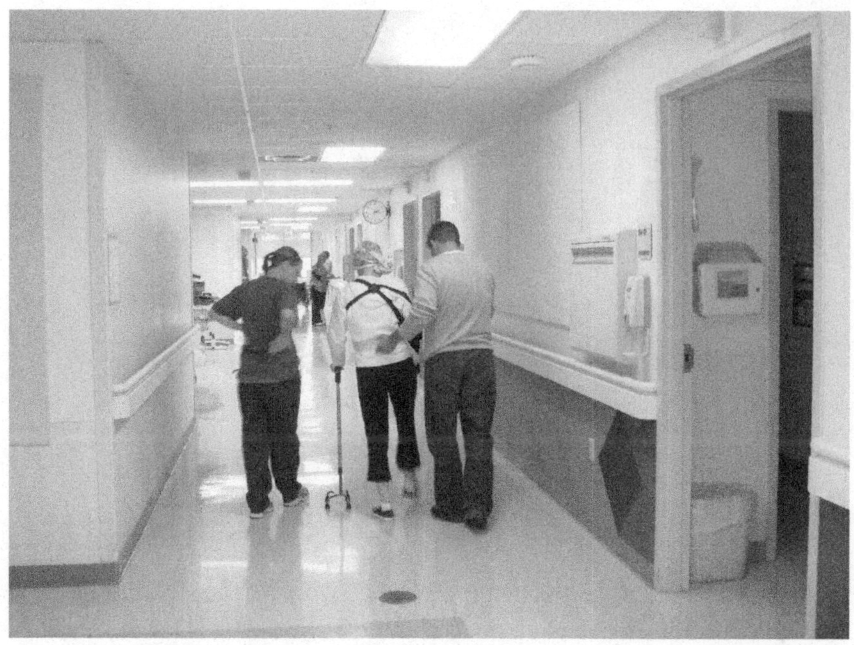

"Her therapy is not over when she leaves our facility," the physician told me. "There will be much more work to be done at home and with outpatient rehab. Kelly can have her outpatient treatment here, but we know that's a long drive for you."

He was right. The rehab facility was forty-five minutes to an hour from home, and our plan was to go to the maximum on outpatient rehab, three days a week. It made more sense to find a facility closer to home. I found one twenty minutes from our house and went to check it out. We didn't know what to expect, just as we hadn't when going to her inpatient facility, but we got to meet with the management team and a couple of therapists and check out all the therapy resources and equipment.

The rehab facility you select depends on what kinds of therapy you will need. An in-person visit is important, because that's how you get a feel for how the facility is run and if it will be the best choice for your success. Questions to consider as you look around should include the following:

- Are the therapists patient yet energetic?
- Is the facility clean? Does it seem somewhat modern?

- Is the facility accredited? The Commission on Accreditation of Healthcare Organizations (CARF) and the Joint Commission on Accreditation of Healthcare Organizations (JCAHO) set standards for quality.
- Are the therapists certified? What other types of professionals are affiliated with the rehab facility (psychiatrists, PTs, OTs, speech therapists, etc.)?
- Is there a plan to monitor progress?
- Does it have a good reputation? When people aren't satisfied or when there's a problem, word can spread.
- Does the facility seem open to involving family members in the treatment plan?

We selected a smaller facility with fewer patients and policies to deal with but experienced and energizing therapists. I thought this would be perfect for her because she could get to know her therapists personally and have a consistent team working with her. I knew this would be important for Kelly to be comfortable and organize her own schedule. Of course, she would need to be the final judge, but I was 99 percent sure she would like it.

"It's smaller, more intimate," I told Kelly later that day. "They don't have tons of patients, and I think you'll get very personalized attention."

With that decided, it was time to figure out what I needed to do at home to adapt to Kelly's needs. Kelly didn't qualify for home health care because she wasn't on any kind of support system and wasn't bedridden. She could get around in a wheelchair. She did, however, qualify for in-home therapy.

An occupational therapist came to the house to make an assessment and helped us figure out what type of equipment and assistive devices we were going to need in the house to adapt to Kelly's situation. For instance, we would need to install grab bars in the shower and near the toilet. She also helped us plan how Kelly could maneuver through the house in her wheelchair.

I tried not to think about how hard it was going to be, and I hoped that just being home would make Kelly better. It was wishful thinking, I know, but then again, a lot of stroke survivors never go home. That we were fortunate enough to have a chance for her to regain her faculties and some sense of her old self was something I would continually remind myself of when her challenges seemed insurmountable.

Kelly

The terror of my image in the mirror was a shock in many ways, but it also served a purpose. It showed me that something really bad had happened. I was also beginning to remember things. Poor Brad. I asked a lot of questions in those days. He was helping me fill in the blanks of my memory.

I wish I could have said, "Brad, you need to remind me who we are, what we do, how we got here, and what happened to me. But you can only tell me one or two things a day. Any more than that, I cannot process."

Of course, I couldn't say any of that, so he was in the dark, and so was I. We had to figure it out through trial and error, so if nothing else, I hope this retelling helps someone else understand how brain injury patients recover. Recovery is putting pieces of a puzzle together for the first time, doing small sections little by little until it all finally connects.

Once I got my skull back on, I focused on doing more therapy. I really did like my therapy. I liked the structure of the schedule, knowing what was going to happen every day at eight, nine, ten, etc.

Next to the nurses' station, a big whiteboard with the master therapy schedule filled a wall. The names of the various occupational, physical, and speech therapists were listed across the top, with the hours of the day down the side. Patients' initials filled the squares of the chart to show the times their therapy would take place.

Every evening, after dinner, I maneuvered myself into my wheelchair. I grabbed my notebook and pen and painstakingly wheeled myself down the hall to the board, using my one good hand. *Left wheel one turn, reach across with left hand, and turn the right wheel one turn.* I had to go slowly, or I would turn the wheelchair in circles, and I had to be constantly aware of where my right arm and leg were so that they wouldn't get caught in the wheel.

Half an hour later, sweaty and out of breath, I'd arrive at the schedule board and search for my initials, KM. When I found my appointments, I would write them all down in my notebook. The nurses at the station all knew me, of course, but no one ever offered to help. They just let me do it on my own, and I guess it was a form of therapy—learning to be independent and make things happen on my own.

Every morning and every evening, in case they had changed the schedule, I would write it down. It wasn't as if I would miss my appointment if I didn't write it down; they were going to come get me when it was time to do therapy. But I'm obsessive about organization and planning my schedule, and even in therapy, I was no different.

My therapists would tell me what I had to do to get out of there, and that became my focus: getting out. "You know more than I do, so just let me know, and I can rah-rah and try to do it," I would say. I was excited about setting my goals, and I had a checklist on which I could mark my progress.

I could get around in my wheelchair, but when I was able to walk with a cane, I felt I had overcome a big hurdle. "Kelly, we need to teach you how to get up when you fall, because you probably will fall at some point," the therapist said.

So I practiced how to get up from the floor. It was kind of like the "Stop, drop, and roll" drill that I'd learned to do in school in case I was ever on fire. I thought about how I could fall onto my left side instead of my right, because that would make it easier to get up, but after a few awkward practice attempts, I instead vowed to myself, "I will not fall!"

It was part of my regimen to get everything organized for the next day. Every evening, after Brad went home, I would take all of my clothes out of the drawers and put them on the bed. I liked to pick out what I would be wearing ahead of time. Then I refolded everything and put it all away. I'm obsessive. That was my personality before, and I was returning to my old self.

As my condition improved, I soon found that I could draw with my left hand. That doesn't seem like much, but it was a big help in communication, because when I couldn't think of the right word, I could draw a picture of what I was trying to say. However, by then, even the words were coming easier, and I had movement in my right hand for the first time since August.

The doctors would stop by occasionally to check on my progress, and they were wonderful people. The nurses were as well—everybody was top notch. Even the evening aides who sat in my bedroom all night in my early days there were 99 percent wonderful. Since the facility cared mostly for older people who'd suffered from strokes, it was different for the staff to have a younger person to work with. There's a different sort of challenge and reward in working with a young person. I feel as if I developed friendships with them, which was gratifying.

The outdoors was also a big part of my healing. I loved the facility's courtyards and the fountain, which Brad and I tossed pennies into to make wishes. It was inspiring, invigorating, and activating to hear the birds, see grass, and even hear traffic and the sounds of the world outside the facility.

Whenever I had a chance, I would say to everybody, "Outside, outside, outside, outside." If it wasn't raining, they would bundle me up and take me out. Even the shortest time outside felt like a gift from God to help keep me going. I could also measure my progress from being wheeled out to walking with a cane with assistance to eventually using my cane on my own.

Outside represented everything that wasn't a hospital or doctor or therapist. Don't get me wrong—I like sterile environments and clean and organized things, but being in that courtyard reminded me that there was more waiting for me outside the walls of my room.

Out of the Comfort Zone

"Good news," the doctor said the morning of October 9. "We're springing you. You're out of here next Friday, October sixteenth."

"Write it on my hand," I told my mom, "so I can see it every day."

I was feeling strong, and I was excited to get out of there, but I was also a little worried. I was still going to do physical therapy when I got home, but it wasn't going to be every day, and I knew that the work and the traveling back and forth would be hard.

I didn't like being in the rehab facility, and I desperately wanted to be home. However, now that the day was approaching, I realized I had gotten pretty comfortable there. The upcoming change was terrifying. *What will it be like when I get home? How are we going to manage? What if my progress stalls without the intense inpatient therapy?* I knew I would have Brad and Mom to help me, but I started to think about all the things I would need to be able to do and about how our house was laid out. I thought about how difficult it would be to navigate all the walls and tight corners with my wheelchair, and we had a sunken living room and steps to the office and basement. We had bar stools with no backs and high-top chairs I could not get in to eat. The laundry was across the house from the bedroom, and we had no railings anywhere. How would I shower and get to the bathroom at night? All these things crossed my mind regarding the day-to-day needs I would have. I would have to count on Brad and Mom to help me. At this point, I was going home whether I was afraid to or not, so I needed to take full advantage of my inpatient therapy, not only doing as much as I could physically but also doing as much as possible for my speech and cognition before I left. I needed something that I could do on my own in my downtime to keep progressing. I was already drawing all the time, and I realized that my mom and family members liked Scrabble. I thought the game might help me, so I talked to my mom about getting Scrabble—except I couldn't remember the word *Scrabble* or the word *tile*. I just repeated "Those things," and I drew a little picture of a tile. I thought it was perfectly clear, but apparently it was not, because it took an hour for her to understand what I meant. She would try to guess what I was drawing: "This? That?" And I would say, "No!" It was like high-stakes charades.

Finally, she figured it out and came through with some tiles. My first word was C-A-T.

Yes! I'm doing it!

We didn't have the whole batch of tiles, and sometimes I'd get frustrated while looking for a letter we didn't have. But soon I could spell *mom*, and eventually, I was able to write lots of words with the tiles, such as *dog*, *me*, *boy*, *girl*, and *dad*. Each word was a small victory but a victory nonetheless, and it was the beginning of my feeling as if I could get better.

The Test-Drive

Before I could go home, I had my first outing, to Walgreens. They wanted to gauge how I would react in public, to see if I was comfortable enough to say hi to somebody who didn't know the situation.

It was surreal to be on the outside, as if I had been in jail and now was out. I hadn't been in a car in months, only ambulances and EMT vehicles, and the experience felt weird and more than a little scary but exhilarating at the same time. It was nice just to be out in a real car, not an ambulance or a shuttle, and then I remembered I needed to get my seat belt on myself. This task was not as easy as a lefty, and I couldn't see the buckle on the right without maneuvering, but I finally got it.

I was all business inside the store, knowing I would be graded on my performance. *Get in and get out, Kel,* I thought to myself. I wasn't worried about my walk with the granny cane, my bald head under the ball cap, my lack of makeup, or other people looking at me. I just wanted to find what was on my list, check out, pay with cash, and get out of there.

I was excited to buy some thank-you notes for all the people who had mailed cards and gifts. I walked in; I had my money. I beelined to the cards. Then I looked up and saw Brad standing at the end of the aisle.

He knew I was coming, and he was spying on me.

I thought to myself, *Brad, you are so bad. Seriously? Hi. I see you there. Don't be all up in my business. I'm going to get a grade for this, so go away.*

But all I could say out loud was "No!"

In spite of my dear spy, I stayed focused on my goals and selected all the cards I wanted. The brain is amazing and frustrating at the same time. Even though my right eye wasn't working yet, I was able to scan the shelf for the style of thank-you cards I liked, look at them to at least get the gist of what they said, and pick my favorite. Then came the challenge of doing the calculation to pay with cash and coins. I could count, but saying the price and checking whether I had the right change was difficult. I could see the numbers in my head and do the math, but I couldn't say the numbers out loud or ask for the amount to check it. Thankfully, the cashier was nice enough to help me through it. I put three dollar bills on the counter and about a dollar in coins.

She said, "You have too much," and she pushed back what I didn't need.

I tried to say, "Thank you," but I'm not sure that's what came out.

She nodded and smiled. I was paid up.

It occurred to me that I might not have been her first shopper from the rehab facility. I carefully picked up my change one coin at a time with my one hand and put it in my wallet. Then I grabbed my bag in my hand with my cane and made my way slowly through the automatic doors. I remember being relieved to make it out on my own, and Brad said I was smiling when I came through the doors.

I knew I hadn't performed perfectly, but still, I had done well enough to earn a passing grade from the therapist, and that was what mattered.

I said to myself, *Okay, I can check that off the list.* I like checking things off lists, if I haven't mentioned that before. That's my ritual, and it felt good.

With that simple yet not-so-simple shopping trip, I was ready to go home and face the outside world again.

If We Only Knew: Going Home

- Map out a daily routine. It's important to think through all the little things that happen throughout an average day and think about whether your home is equipped to facilitate these activities. An occupational therapist has a special role in stroke rehabilitation. His or her expertise includes identifying modifications to an environment to accomplish a task, identifying accommodative technologies, developing strategies, and assisting with evaluations. An occupational therapist will usually visit your home and recommend adaptations before you are released. If that is not the case for your facility, request the visit anyway.

- Think about basic safety. Install grab bars in the shower and around toilets, and add railings on the stairs and places where the wheelchair or cane will not be stable. You need a checklist to identify safety risks and assess upgrades needed, including wheelchair access, railings, stools and chairs, temporary or permanent grab bars in the bathroom and shower, steps required, mirrors and sinks, cabinets and tables, and a way to get to vehicles from the house. Develop this checklist in conjunction with your occupational and physical therapists.

- Find a medical supply store. There's probably one near you. Maybe you had no idea it was there. Such a store will have canes, wheelchairs, grab bars, braces, motorized scooters, walkers, and most anything you need. Most importantly, it will lease most large items for as long as you need them, and the lease should be covered by your health insurance. Your health savings account is a great asset too.

- Be aware of right- or left-side neglect danger. The biggest danger in the house other than a fall will be the patient's lack of recognition and sensation of the side of his or her body affected by the stroke. He or she can trap an arm or leg in doors or drawers; burn him- or herself on the stove; drop knives, plates, and pans; and bang into doorknobs and walls. Neglect typically also includes vision-field cuts wherein a patient only sees half of what's in front of him or her. You need to consider all these conditions before you get home so that any dangers can be mitigated.

- You will need help at home. You will likely get all kinds of offers from friends and family, but be realistic. They might be well intentioned, but you could need daily assistance with the most basic things, and most won't have the flexibility to be there when you need them. Who will really be ready and able? Make a short list, and be transparent about what tasks will likely be involved.

- Look into personal errand and concierge services. Google them in your area, and start doing some homework. They make a huge difference and can be affordable if you focus on weekly recurring things, such as groceries, organization around the house, and rides to appointments.

- Be prepared for a recurrence. Be sure to understand whether or not a recurrence is likely, and if it is, know what the symptoms might look like. If you are a seizure risk, ask your doctors how to prepare for the unlikely event so that you don't panic. Seizures are a common possibility for stroke survivors and can look scary if you aren't prepared.

- Consider what is important to the patient. For Kelly, getting outside meant a lot. Plan to do those favorite activities often to comfort and encourage the survivor.

- Know the pharma regimen. Have the pharmacology instructions written down and electronically available. Know what each drug does and what the goal is in terms of ongoing care or slowly reducing the schedule to zero. Understand warning signs that reduction is too fast and side effects of improper dosage. Keep everything together in your file so that anyone on your recovery team can access and read the information.

CHAPTER 8

Home Is Where the Heart Is

Kelly

A couple of days before going home, I said, "I would like to have therapy in the morning on the day I'm leaving."

The nurse looked at me in surprise. "Nobody ever wants to do that."

"Well, I want to. I want to say that I've done that and check it off the list." I had to know I had done absolutely everything I could before going home.

I was ready to go home, until it was actually time. The night before my discharge, I lay awake, thinking and worrying. *What am I going to do? It's a different regimen, and I don't know how I can do it on my own and keep making progress.* Going home was a huge and scary step. I was excited and petrified all at once, but there was no turning back now.

I had mixed emotions when the nurse helped me from my wheelchair into Brad's car in front of the facility, and I said a bittersweet good-bye to the people who'd helped save my life and start to rebuild it. I didn't have the words to thank everyone; I hoped they could see from the tears in my eyes how much I appreciated all they had done for me.

Brad and I rode in anxious silence during the forty-five-minute drive home; my heart was racing, and my face felt flushed. As we neared our house, my anxiety peaked.

"Brad," I said, "it's real."

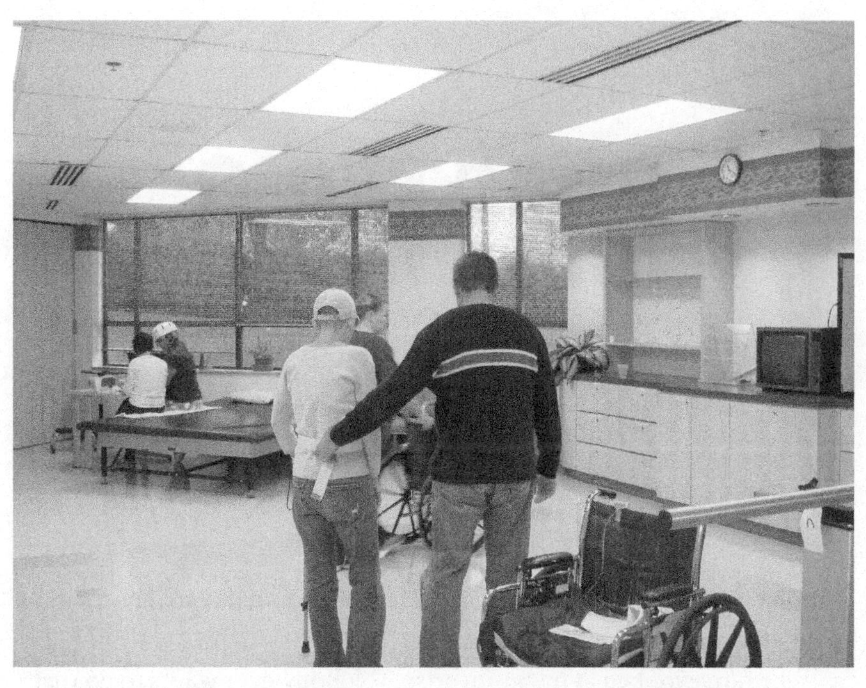

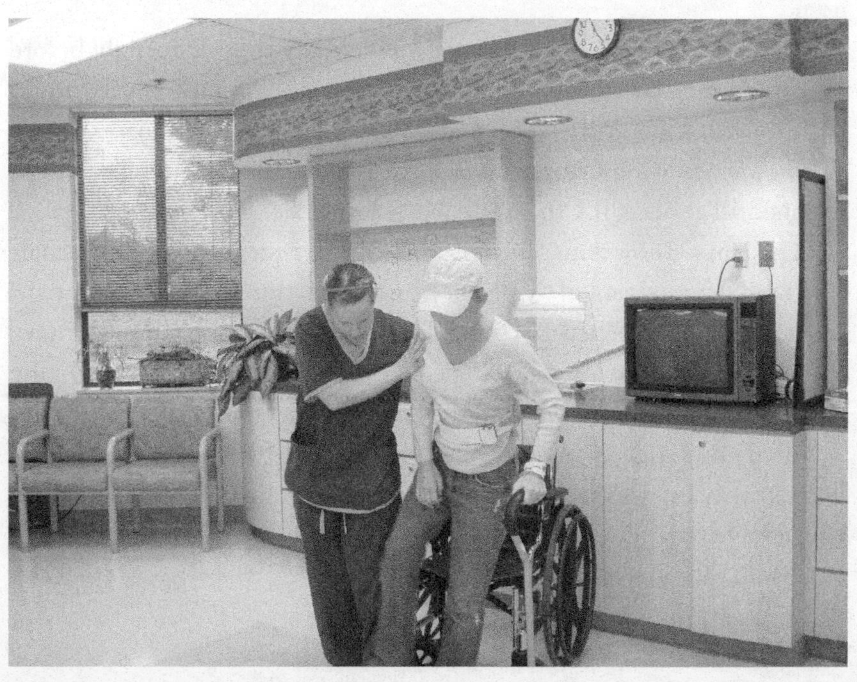

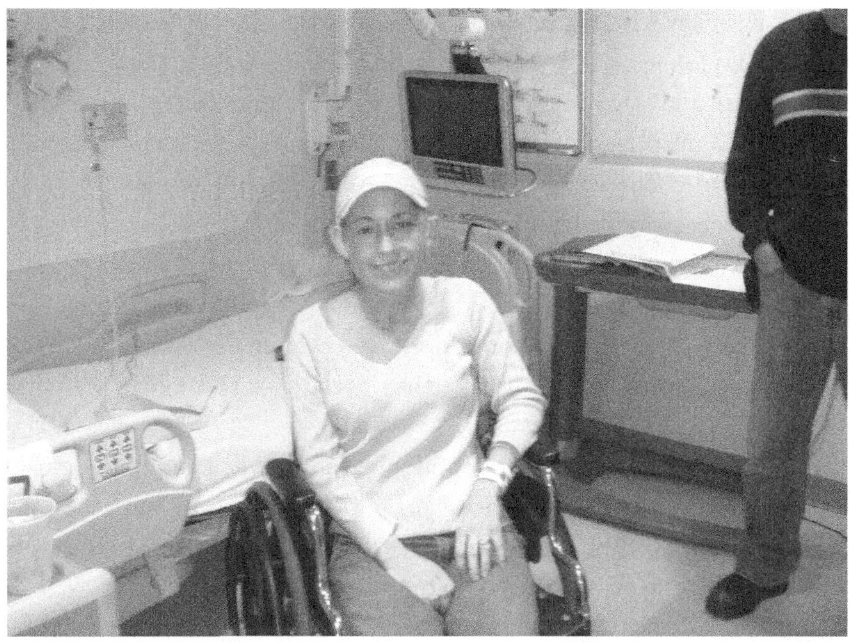

He knew what I was feeling. I was worried about leaving my protective bubble and afraid to see all those neighbors I knew casually. I almost felt ashamed. I had always thought of myself as tough, and I wasn't tough anymore. I had always been independent, and now I could barely do anything on my own. Who was I now that I wasn't that person?

As we turned the corner, I saw a banner outside our house. "Welcome Home, Kelly!" it proclaimed. My breathing became shallow. The banner was right there by our driveway, where everyone could see it. A colleague from work who had been wonderful to me, bringing paper and pens for me to use in therapy, had printed the sign.

It was a wonderful, generous gesture. I hated it.

Brad read my mood. "I know you don't want that sign up, Kelly," Brad said. "I'm sorry. We'll take it down."

I knew they meant well, but just coming home was enough for me. I didn't want a parade. I just wanted quiet.

My mom and dad were waiting on the front step, their faces a strange mixture of joy and fearful anticipation. Brad helped me out of the car and into the wheelchair and rolled me up to the steps, where I put my wheelchair dismount-and-stand-up training into practice right away. *Lock my chair.*

Check. Brace my left arm, and lift myself up with Brad's help on my harness. Check. Good foot up the step with my cane and then weaker foot. Check. I had to think ahead and plan every move to be safe and stable. The front steps and doorway to our home were immediate challenges, which foreshadowed things to come. But we made it inside, one small step at a time.

The house was filled with flowers and cards sent by family and friends who didn't know what else to do. *We have a lot of thank-you notes to write* was the first thought that crossed my mind.

"We're so happy you're home, honey!" my mom exclaimed. "Dad has been so busy around the house, getting it ready for you. Come see what he's done!"

I got back in my wheelchair and wheeled slowly around my house, struggling to move the chair forward on the carpet and bumping into walls and doors right out of the gate. It was overwhelming, to put it mildly, and we were already going to need some touch-up paint.

"Look at the bathroom. There are grab bars to help you get into the shower." She pointed to a small white seat. "There's a bench for you to sit on while you shower." I could see that my dad was proud of the work he had done, happy to be able to contribute. I tried to be appreciative of their efforts, but I'm sure my face told the truth—that I was still coming to terms with the fact that I would not be independent again for a long time.

Room by room, I rolled through the house that Brad and I had designed together just a year ago. I knew every inch of that house by heart. I had chosen every light fixture and door handle. But it didn't feel like home anymore.

I thought to myself, *Am I dreaming? Where am I? It's all familiar, but I can't use the furniture or get into all the rooms.* My mind raced like the Energizer Bunny. *What will we do? How will I get around these tight hallways? There are no railings, and our living room is sunken. How will I do the laundry? How will I use the high-top kitchen stools? How will I use the shower and bathroom? Who will help? And everyone expects me to be my old self and do what I did.* It was all too much, and I wished I was back at the hospital. It seemed as if I had been gone for years, and now everything was different, and I still couldn't speak well enough to express my fears to Brad.

I needed to take a breath and rest just so I wouldn't have another stroke. I think Brad and Mom knew from my expression and the tears welling up in my eyes that I was scared, and they probably were too. They both said, "Don't worry; it will be okay," which echoed one of my favorite aphasia lines that I said for everything: "going to be okay." I guess I had trained them well after all. It was only early afternoon, but Brad helped me to our bedroom and gently to my pillow, kissed me, and told me he would check on me. Reassured for the moment, I got some much-needed rest and convinced myself that tomorrow would be a new day. I was home.

Home Visiting Hours

Other things I hadn't been prepared for were hosting visitors and dealing with social situations, but that was exactly what we did the first weekend. There wasn't any preparation in therapy for that, and we probably didn't realize how challenging it would be for me. Everyone had been waiting to see me, and they all wanted to show their support and love, so we hated to tell people to stay away. I hadn't seen my aunts and uncles, and my cousin was in town from Florida. They all stopped by, which was nice, at least for a few minutes. But just as in the rehab center, I was easily overstimulated by people and noise, and as soon as they arrived, I found myself wishing they would leave. My appearance was pretty normal considering what I had been through; I just had a little less hair, and I had lost some weight. What they couldn't see was that my brain wasn't normal and was still healing, so all the stimulation was not a good thing.

We got through it, and we were still figuring it out as we went. We had to learn how to balance family and friends with what my brain could take. I don't remember much, but I remember it was a beautiful day, and I was relieved to know that people still wanted to be around me.

Although they normally spent their winters in Florida, my mom and dad remained at their summer house on the river, about twenty minutes away. I still wasn't walking on my own, and I was at risk for a fall, so I needed to have someone with me at all times. Mom was moving in.

Full Circle

The next week, we had an assessment at our outpatient rehab facility. "You know, Kelly," Brad said as he parked the car, "this building is right across the street from the hospital where we spent the first night after the stroke." He pointed across the street. "We've come full circle."

I liked the facility right away. A bubbly, smiling receptionist welcomed us, and the lead therapist for my case introduced me to the others and gave me a tour of the physical and occupational therapy areas. She explained the technology and how the process would work. I was pleasantly surprised at how young the therapists were and felt immediately at home in the bright but peaceful environment.

Maybe this will work after all.

"We have you scheduled for three days a week, three hours at a time," the lead therapist told us. "We'll start next Tuesday."

I was ready. It was going to be another week before I could get started, which worried me a bit. I wanted to get going right away; otherwise, I'd be anxious and feel as if I were losing that time.

"It's okay, Kelly," Brad said, trying to calm me, as usual. "We have things we need to do to get you settled at home and to prepare for therapy. Don't worry about it. It's not a setback."

I was checking things that were happening off my list. *Okay,* I thought, *therapy is set. Mom is settled in, so Brad can work. The house is ready. This is good.*

It was great to have my mom with me. No one knew me like my mom did. She knew all my personality quirks, my tendency to obsess—all of it. Brad could go back to work and really focus, knowing I was being well taken care of.

We had a lot of fun doing girl stuff together, such as shopping. I had lost enough weight that my clothes didn't fit, and besides, I needed things that were easier to pull on and off and that would work well for therapy—no more button-downs or pullovers. So Mom took me shopping, and soon I had enough clothing, at least for the short term.

I think she was nervous though. While I was still in rehab, she had participated in a few caregiver training sessions with Brad to learn how to help me walk with an assisting strap, go up and down stairs, get in and out of my chair, and help me up if I fell. She had to know how to secure me so that I wouldn't fall. The strap, or harness, looked like a belt that wrapped around both of us, allowing her to support me with her whole body instead of just her arms. Brad was strong enough to help me walk without the strap, but my mom is small, and using it made her feel more secure.

Daily Life Becomes an Obstacle Course

While I worked in rehab to improve my shaky balance, I used the wheelchair to move around the house or at the store. I could navigate small areas, such as the kitchen, myself by using a cane and holding on to furniture or the island for support and balance.

We had some stools by the island, and I would perch on a stool, thinking I was sitting stably, when all of a sudden—*crash!*—I would fall. Since I could feel my butt on the left side but not on the right, I didn't realize I wasn't sitting all the way on the stool. Or I would get on the stool, scoot backward, and fall right off the other side.

"Okay, I need to remember that," I noted.

"Maybe you should sit in the kitchen chairs that have backs on them," my mom suggested helpfully.

There were other small obstacles in the house. For example, we had a sunken living room. It was just one step down, but that meant I couldn't roll around the entire first floor. I found ways to navigate the wheelchair to the edge of the area, set the brake, and then use my cane and hold on to furniture to take one step down with my left foot.

Our master bedroom was on the first floor, which was a blessing. The shower was relatively easy to manage with the help of my mom or Brad. If I needed to go to the restroom in the middle of the night, which I always did, it was easy to position the cane right by my bedside. I would stand up using the cane and then swivel to the wheelchair.

Brad would always wake up and help me because it was a little tight in the bathroom with the wheelchair, and I needed help getting from the wheelchair to the toilet and back. For at least the first week, I would nudge him awake, saying, "I need to go." Eventually, I got a little bit braver, and I progressed pretty quickly to being able to take care of my nighttime needs independently.

Luckily, my balance improved quickly with therapy, and I bid good riddance to the wheelchair after about three weeks. I was working hard to get more mobile and confident so that I could be more independent and so that Brad would worry less about a fall. A bad fall was really the only thing that could set me back at that point. If I sprained something or broke a bone now, I would miss my six- to nine-month recovery window that was so important to us. We couldn't let that happen.

The Fitch

Speech and cognition continued to be my biggest challenges. Often, I felt as if Brad and I were playing Twenty Questions instead of having a conversation.

C'mon. C'mon. What is this? What is this? What is this? I'd think while Brad tried to guess what I was referring to. I still substituted words, sometimes even making up my own words.

One day, on the drive back from therapy, I was telling Brad that I did not want to see a friend who had asked to come by. She had been my friend since we were babies, and I hadn't seen her since the stroke, but I just didn't feel up to a visit.

"Brad, I'm such a fitch," I said.

"Fitch?" he said.

"Yes. C'mon, Brad. I'm such a fitch."

He was smiling, choking back a laugh. "You mean a bitch?"

"Yes, that's what I said. A fitch."

"Kelly, you're saying *fitch*, but you mean *bitch*."

"Yes, fitch," I said, and suddenly, we were both laughing about our new private joke.

Because if you can't laugh, I mean, c'mon.

Years later, the fitch story still gives us a laugh and is a great reminder of my will to recover. In fact, it almost made the cut as the book title, but *Love Stroke* won out in the end.

Life of the Party—or Not

We still used the CarePages to update our friends and family, and it was a big day when I was able to take over the postings. I labored over the short note, which the old Kelly would have knocked out in just a few minutes, but an hour and a half later and almost sixty days after my stroke, I was able to hit the send button.

October 27, 2009, 6:42 p.m.
Thank You, Everybody

Hey, everybody. I am finally on the CarePages and able to read everyone's messages and Brad's frequent updates.

I have been home for ten days and am getting into a routine. I have been to outpatient rehab three times so far, and it will be good but difficult as I continue to go three times a week for three hours each day. My family has been immensely supportive, especially Mom and Brad, who are daily doing everything to help me make progress. I can't thank all of my friends and family enough for their support over the past eight weeks. It's been a long haul, and every day I will continue to work hard and make progress. I will continue to post updates as I make lots of progress. I look forward to seeing everyone over the next few weeks.

Love you all,
Kelly

My family has always loved Halloween and dressing up in costume, so the family party was a big deal, and Katie was throwing it that year.

"Do you think you'd like to go?" Brad asked me, not really expecting a yes. "We can drive you down the driveway to the door to their basement bar. You won't need to walk down any stairs."

I knew the party would be an effort, but I wanted to fight for Brad because he had fought so hard for me. I thought for a minute before I said, "I'm not going to let this stroke stand in my way. Let's just go; we need to go. We should just go dressed as GI Jane and GI Joe."

This was another private joke—I looked like GI Jane because my hair had not grown back yet. Plus, we certainly felt like warriors.

But where would we get costumes? On the spur of the moment, we decided to try the flea market near our house, wheelchair and all. We had never even been to the flea market but didn't stop to think about it; we just did it. While I was mainly using my cane at home, not knowing the layout of the flea market, we opted to take my wheelchair. We would do that just in case early on, as I couldn't walk far, and if it was a crowded place, people would knock into me. We roamed the flea market for an hour or so and had fun picking out our costumes: fatigues, combat boots, and hats. It was fun but also interesting, as people stared at me in my chair and with my arm sling, no doubt wondering why I was shopping at a flea market in my condition, but they mostly went on their way after seeing me and quickly pretending not to look. They might have thought I was already in a war, which, in a way, I was. I was focused on finding a certain type of boot that I could zip all the way down to get on my bad foot. But of course, I couldn't say the words, so I had to just point at stuff, and Brad would pull it out. I think the flea marketers were a little frustrated with the back and forth, but they wanted the sale. We finally pieced together our uniforms, and off we went. It doesn't seem like much, but the flea market trip symbolized the first of many adventures we likely would not have taken had it not been for my stroke.

So two months from the day of my stroke, Brad and I put on our matching "uniforms" and attended my first family outing. It was cool when we showed up in costume and everyone made a big fuss over me for a few minutes. It was another small victory and a brief moment of normalcy.

After the initial welcome, though, I noticed that people were not talking to me. They talked to each other, and they all talked to Brad about me.

"Brad, Kelly is looking so well!"

"Brad, where did you get these great costumes?"

"Hey, Brad, how is it going at home? How is Kelly feeling?"

It was as if I weren't sitting right there in front of them. That was the first time I experienced what I now call my invisibility.

Seriously, you guys? What the hell is going on? I thought. *Why don't you talk to me?*

But the words didn't come easily or quickly to me, and I found myself checking out after a few minutes, unable to exert the effort required to insert myself into the conversations.

This state of invisibility became something important that I would have to learn to overcome as I progressed in my recovery. I know it's not a technical term, but I guarantee you it's a real feeling for someone who is recovering from a traumatic brain injury or is disabled.

The best way to describe it is a phenomenon in which you are the center of attention or one of the main attractions of other people's concern, discussion, or visual attention, but they all operate as if you aren't even there. This is not a criticism of people but an observation of human nature when disabled people are involved. Invisibility is a concept I've become as comfortable as I can with. I don't get too bothered anymore, but I also make it clear to people that I'm still a person and should be part of any conversation about me.

I just politely say, "I'm here. You can talk to me."

After a couple of hours, Brad took me home, where I could rest my brain. I settled into bed that night and thought about the day and where I had been just two weeks ago. Overall, the party had been fun, and it was great to see everybody, so I let go of the little frustrations and just let myself feel the peace and happiness of being home with Brad, where I belonged.

Throughout my recovery so far, my therapists and doctors had said over and over, "You've made remarkable progress. You're a fighter, so if you want it, you can do it."

I believed that I could do it, that I would get back to my former self and be able to live my old life. That was my goal, and I was working toward it with determination.

It was good to be home.

If We Only Knew: Visitors at Home

- Ensure all the items on the homecoming checklist are complete. Safety first!

- Be sure to take advantage of any caregiver training sessions before returning home and after, if appropriate. Caregiver support groups not only are a wonderful break but also can give you ideas you haven't thought about and help identify resources you didn't know existed.

- Don't have a party. We made this mistake. Patients need to slowly get used to their houses again and get comfortable at their own pace. Although everyone wants to see them, they can likely take only a few visitors at a time over several weeks. The best thing friends and family can do is be patient.

- Manage stimuli. When visitors do come, they should talk softly and slowly and not all at the same time. The brain is still learning to process information and cannot keep up with one conversation, much less multiple conversations at once.

- Rest. Rest is still important for the stroke survivor. Don't be afraid to tell visitors that the survivor needs to rest and that it's time to go.

- Be aware of the invisibility phenomenon. People won't mean to talk about the patient in front of him or her, but they will. Either talk to the survivor directly and patiently, or don't talk about him or her at all. Brad would point people to me when they would ask about me in front of me. Eventually, people figure it out, but it's hard, as they want quick and detailed responses, which are impossible. They need to save all the medical questions for another time and be happy just seeing and spending time with the survivor.

- Be careful in crowds. Due to the lack of sensation, patients will not realize when people are going to bump into them in a crowd on their weak side and will walk right into them since they cannot see or feel them.

- Prepare the visitors. If you can let the visitors know the importance of the above information ahead of arrival, it will help them and the survivor be comfortable and make the most of their time together. It can be awkward on both sides if expectations aren't set ahead of time.

CHAPTER 9

It's Up to Us Now

Kelly

All the doctors had said the first six months were make or break, the big window for making the most progress, so I used that as motivation, and my goal became to do as much as possible in that six-month window. I was excited to get started on the new stage of therapy.

Outpatient therapy began with assessments and a discussion of my goals. I set short- and long-term goals for each type of therapy. It was all about balance and strength training. I needed to be comfortable walking on my own without assistance, even though I did not have feeling or motor skills in my right arm and hand and my right leg and foot were not working well yet.

I had to help my brain build new pathways to these simple tasks, always with the chance that it might not work. I spent hours just learning to go up and down the stairs. It sounds simple, but when you cannot feel or control your right foot, leg, arm, and hand, it is challenging and dangerous.

I was getting a lesson in all the things I used to take for granted. It was hard work, but it never got tedious, because I could see myself making progress every single day, which made it easy to keep my motivation up.

The occupational therapy was a little tougher, and the speech therapy was the hardest for me. The progress in these areas was slower, but still, every day I felt I was accomplishing something, and that kept me going.

They wouldn't allow me to do outpatient therapy more than three times a week, but we hired a personal trainer to come to the house to do additional strength training. I was determined to do as much as I possibly could, while being careful not to overwork my muscles, which needed time to recover between training sessions.

Occupational therapy included a lot of working with balls, playing catch, and working to open and close my right hand so that I could grasp objects. I had, and still have, a lot of spasticity in my right arm. Spasticity is a common challenge for stroke survivors, and the best way to describe it is a constant charley horse in your arm or leg. The brain sends electronic signals to your extremities that contract your biceps, calf muscle, and finger and toe tendons. Because you don't control it, it overpowers your normal arm and leg neurology and causes the deformities in how you carry your arm or how you walk. Spasticity is why you see stroke survivors walk with drop foot or a limp and have a hinged arm.

I worked with an electronic stimulation machine (e-stim) that wrapped around my arm to help my nerves remember how to extend my fingers, release, and grip. The machine would override the spasticity and allow me to relearn proper motion. It was an amazing machine that I had never known existed. I practiced my fine motor skills using those triangular games with the pegs, the ones they have at Cracker Barrel. I'd move one peg at a time over and over until I could finish the sequence within a certain amount of time. Then I could move on to the next task. Repetition is the only way to relearn these motions that are critical to everyday tasks. It didn't look like much, but it was equivalent to running a marathon for my brain, tendons, and muscles, which had been asleep for weeks.

All along the way, there were tests to pass and goals to reach to progress to the next stage of therapy. I remembered how excited we had all been when my nieces and nephews learned to pinch with their forefingers and thumbs to eat Cheerios. Now I was in the same boat. It is amazing how many daily activities you can do if you can just pinch. Try going through a day without that capability in your dominant hand.

My goal for speech therapy was to speak in full sentences. I had issues with vocabulary, verb tenses, pronouns, and remembering the names of some objects. The speech therapist would hold up a flash card, and I would see it and know what it was, but I couldn't articulate the correct word. To be unable to express the thought that was in my head was the most frustrating experience for me.

Speech therapy was my "Woe is me" time. I didn't feel I was progressing as much as I should have or as much as I wanted to. I studied as much as possible on my own. My mom made flash cards for me, and we worked on them together. We did word puzzles and anything we could think of to help my language skills.

I'm a visual learner; seeing something written down helps me to remember it. If somebody said something I needed to remember, I would say, "Okay, I need to write this down in my folder, because then I can learn it." For me, it worked in three steps:

1. Say it.
2. Write it.
3. Read it.

That was my method, and I used it over and over again until I could remember the word. If I couldn't remember it, I would open my folder and read it again.

I still use this method to learn new words and names, and it works every time.

Did I mention that I had to learn to write left-handed? Well, I did, because thanks to the spasticity I talked about earlier and my lack of feeling, I would never hold a pen in my right hand again, at least not with the dexterity needed to print or write. I had taken the first steps toward left-handedness in the rehab facility and by now had come to terms with this reality. I practiced relentlessly, and nowadays, my left-handed writing is better than Brad's right-handed writing.

One of my therapists explained the brain's process of rebuilding pathways to us in a simple way: "Imagine that one day, on your drive to the grocery store, the road is suddenly closed. You know there's another route to get you there, but you don't have navigation or a map, and it's a trial-and-error process to find the shortest route that works." Eventually, the brain can remap the path to the store, but the new path might not be as fast as the old one. This idea helped us understand what my brain was going through and why there was hope to relearn everyday functions.

NO STEP

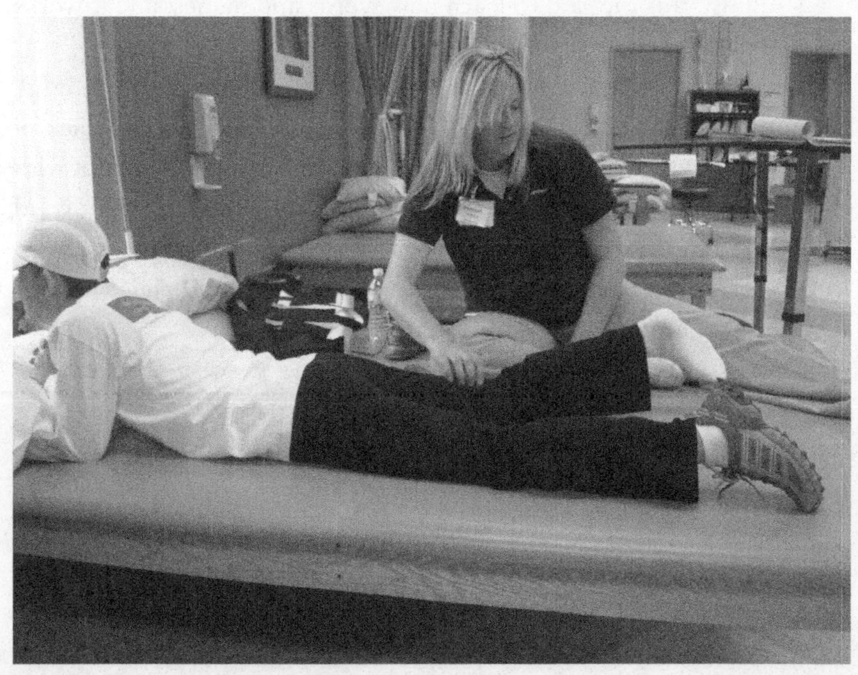

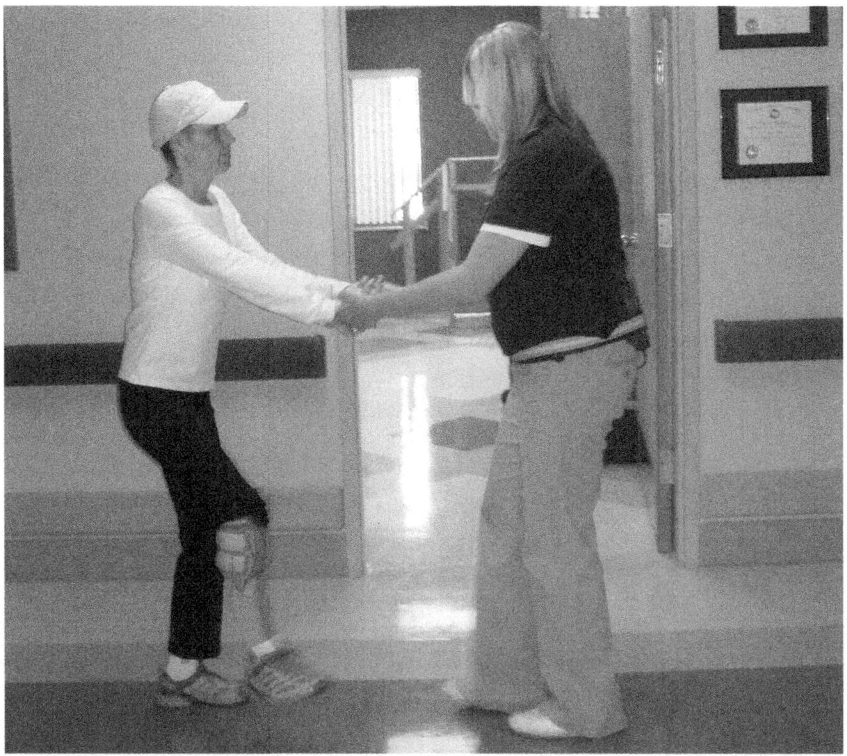

Sensible Shoes

Everything went according to plan for a couple of weeks. I felt I was improving, but every once in a while, I just needed to cry.

Those times when I melted down could also be comical. One time I was in our bathroom after my shower. "Mom!" I called out to her. "I have a lot of jeans. I need to try on all my jeans and throw out the ones that don't fit. I need to purge a little bit."

"Oh, come on, Kelly," my mom said. "Do we really need to do that right now?"

"Yes, I want to do it now. I don't need all that stuff. If it doesn't work now, I don't think it ever will. I might as well get rid of it."

One by one, with my mom's help, I tried on every pair of jeans in my closet—GAP, Lucky, boot-cut, straight-leg, dark-wash, stone-wash, and black jeans. I loved those jeans, and they used to look great on me. Now they hung like flour sacks.

"See? I look ridiculous in these," I said, my voice cracking. I remembered all the times I had shimmied into those jeans and a slinky top, showing off my fit figure. "I can't believe I can't wear any of my clothes!" I cried. "This isn't fair. At all."

"Well, think of how much fun you're going to have buying all new clothes," my mom said cautiously, not sure how I would react.

My tears turned to laughter as I pictured trying on jeans in a department store dressing room. "Honestly, Mom, how in the world is that ever going to happen?" I laughed.

Getting rid of all my beloved shoes was another milestone in my new normal. Like a lot of women, I loved shoes in general and high heels in particular. My closet was packed with a hundred pairs of shoes, stored neatly in their boxes, arranged by color and style.

However, early on, it became clear that I would never again wear heels. From now on, it would be sensible and stable shoes for me. Along with my shoes, I had lost clothes with certain kinds of buttons or zippers and much of my jewelry.

When you realize that your new life cannot include many of the things you love, it sucks. There's no other way to say it. You have to find a way to appreciate what you *can* do and what you still have rather than focusing on what you've lost.

It was painful, but I finally decided I needed to overhaul my wardrobe. No matter how much I wished a lot of my old clothes and heels would work for me, I knew it was not likely to happen, and looking at the unwearable clothing and shoes every day was too frustrating for me. So I had an idea for a free closet sale at our house for my aunts, nieces, friends, colleagues, and their kids. It ended up being like a fun fashion show where I got to see family and friends, and it was nice stuff—a lot of stuff. To this day, I still smile when I see my family members and their kids wearing my clothes and know that I managed to turn a painful process for me into a positive one. The other good news was that the clothing purge made room for my new one-armed and therapy-skewed wardrobe.

Adaptive clothing is available from specialty stores or online retailers, such as Amazon. Adaptive clothing is made with the needs of the user in mind. For example, when you sit in a wheelchair, you need pants that come up far enough in the back, and regular pants might not be cut that way. You might need a top that's open in the back so that it's easy to put on or easy for a caregiver to remove, and even though the top slips over your head, it might have faux buttons to look like a button-down shirt. Adaptive clothing often uses Velcro closures and might have hidden panels or back openings. There are many adaptive clothing companies, and you can Google them to get an idea of what you might need. You can buy stylish, nice clothes almost anywhere when you know what to look for.

- For therapy, you'll want comfortable clothes that aren't too loose or too tight. Yoga pants, jogging pants, T-shirts, and sweatshirts are appropriate.

- If you are a woman, you might also need to reevaluate all of your bras. It might be too hard to use them if they hook in the back. You'll need front-closure bras that close with Velcro or snaps.

- Because grip strength is often affected at least on one side, button-down shirts and blouses are out. Think about shirts with a wide neck or a V-neck that are easy to slip over the head and easy to put your arms in (no tugging!). Cardigans might be difficult to put on, especially if they're tight in the sleeves, but some faux cardigan sets can give you the warmth of layers without the need to put on an additional layer, because the shirt and cardigan are one unit that pulls over your head.

- In general, partial zippers are okay as long as the zipper slides easily and the pull is wide or is a ring so that you can grip it. There are adaptations (zipper pullers) that can attach to the zipper, making it easier to operate with limited strength.

- Pants should have elastic waistbands, which are easier to pull up and down than something with a button and a small zipper. Loose-fitting pants are important for therapy, but the pants cannot drag on the ground (which is a tripping hazard) and need to be the right length.

- Socks can be challenging if you have mobility issues. There are sock aids that make a rigid form for the sock, which is then pulled over the foot. If you'd like to buy one, Google *dressing aids*.

- Shoes need to slip on or have Velcro closures, but you might also be able to use elastic laces, which snap rather than tie. It goes without saying that the heel has to be low for balance. Long-handled shoehorns are another great adaptive tool to help slide the foot into the shoe so that you don't have to bend. Be sure the shoe fits well, because a loose shoe can cause you to trip.

- There are belts designed to operate with one hand. If belts are needed, the belts should be threaded through the pants before the pants are worn. You might want to buy one belt for each pair of pants so that no one has to keep changing the belt every time you need one.

- Accessories are not completely out of the picture, if you decide you want to wear them at some point. However, you'll have to consider the practicality of these as well, and most of the time, you might find they are more effort than they're worth. You might not be able to put in earrings and might need someone to do it for you. Necklaces that slip over your head and bracelets that slip onto your hand might still work for you, and there are adaptive grippers that can help you slide them on and off. Preknotted scarves that slip over your head can add a splash of color if you feel that's important.

- With regard to grooming, there are many adaptive tools for grooming, including standing hairdryer stands so that you don't have to hold the dryer, mitts with pockets for soap so that you don't have to squeeze soap (which is wet and slippery) onto the mitt in the shower, handheld showers so that you can control the shower spray, toothpaste squeezers, nail brushes with suction cups so that you can clean your nails one-handed, and so on. There are also dining aids, and your OT can suggest many of these. Try Google if you've identified a particular need. Someone has probably invented a product to make your life easier.

When I wasn't at therapy, there were some exercises we could do at home, mostly related to stretching and range of motion. Brad helped me with those, because my mom was afraid she would hurt me.

My mom's area was the fun, girlie stuff, such as painting my nails and plucking my eyebrows. We watched a lot of movies too. My mom handled all the laundry, and together we wrote a lot of thank-you notes. I couldn't write them myself, so I would say, "I want to say thank you to Aunt and Uncle. Figure it out." I still couldn't speak completely in full sentences, but my mom knew what I meant.

Together my mom and I managed the flow of visitors. I was excited to see my best friend, Megan, who hadn't been allowed to see me in rehab. Cathy, my boss and friend, also paid me visits. I napped several times a day and still took a lot of medication. My pillbox looked like my grandma's and grandpa's had before they passed away; I couldn't believe how many pills I had to take. While the amount is way down from those early days, I still take five or six pills in the morning and before bed, and it will be that way forever, but when it comes to antiseizure pills, taking them is better than the alternative.

As with many other aspects of my new life, I didn't like it, but I had to suck it up and deal with it.

Miracle Machine

My toes were scrunched, and I had foot drop from the spasticity, which meant I had trouble lifting the front of my foot off the ground with my ankle (dorsiflexion) when I walked to create the correct heel-toe motion. This caused me to drag my toes and often stub them, which created problems for my balance.

A common treatment for foot drop is an orthotic, or boot, called an ankle-foot orthosis, which holds the foot in the appropriate position so that you don't stumble when you pull your leg through to take a step. I hated the AFO because it was uncomfortable, and I needed to wear specific shoes with it.

Brad and I started doing some research into a better solution. I was beginning to use a computer again for e-mail and the Internet. Brad found the Young Stroke Survivor website at youngstroke.org, which became a great resource for us.

It was there we discovered an experimental new biostimulation device called a WalkAide, designed for people with food drop as a result of traumatic brain injury, stroke, multiple sclerosis, and cerebral palsy. It leverages functional electrical stimulation (FES) to restore nerve-to-muscle signals when you take a step and, thus, improves walking ability.

I found one physical therapist in Cincinnati who worked with WalkAides, so we went to have a discussion and see if I would qualify for using it. The device doesn't work in people with nerve damage. My nerves work, but the purposeful signals from my brain don't reach my foot because of the spasticity, so it was perfect for me.

I tried it in the orthopedics office, and it was amazing. The WalkAide has two electrodes, set so that when I took a step forward, it raised my toes up and out, so I had a heel strike when my foot landed, without my having to hike up my hip to pull my foot through, as I had been doing. It doesn't require corrective shoes—it just taped to my leg and allowed me to walk with a normal gait. I could wear it under clothes and almost feel normal again.

It was like a miracle machine. I wore it constantly in those early months. When I wore it, my stability and confidence were 100 percent improved, and my limp wasn't as severe. While too late for us, I am happy to say that I think five years later, insurance does cover these devices if you have a loved one in need.

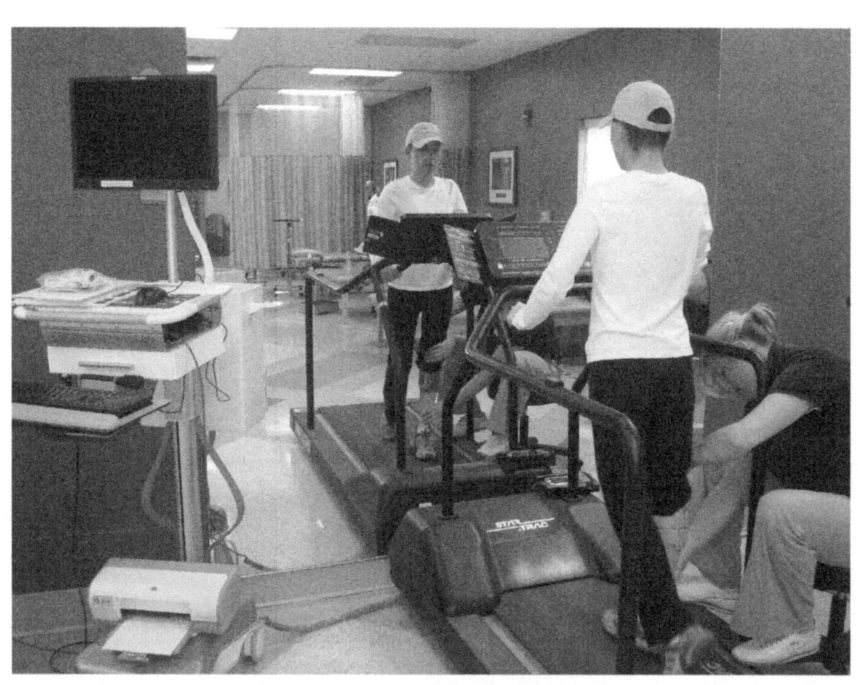
STAR TRAC

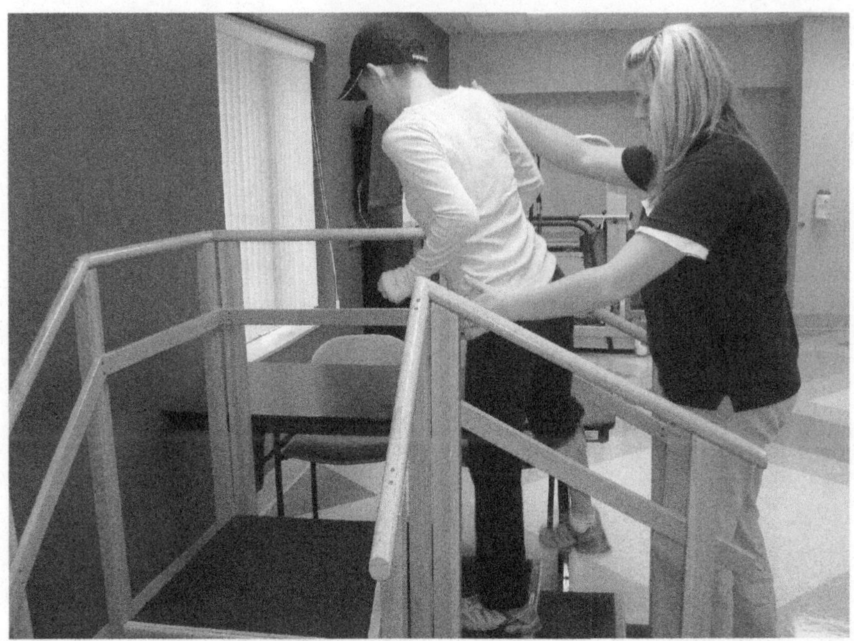

Hope for the Holidays

After a few weeks at home, I reached the point of feeling blessed every day, which hadn't always been the case. I decided to trust my faith and focus on the future. Brad had been amazing, staying by my side every step of the way and keeping me positive and focused on my goals. I realized how fortunate I was to have my family and friends offering constant support and well-wishes.

Everyone should have a problem as terrible as having to keep people who love you away.

About a month after my homecoming, return visits to the doctors confirmed what we believed: therapy was going well. Each doctor was impressed with my progress, and my neurosurgeon even said I was "well ahead of the curve."

"That's what I'm talking about," I said as I reached out to spontaneously shake his hand with my right hand—the hand I'd been unable to move only weeks ago. He had not seen me since he'd reattached my skull plate and put the fifty-two stitches in my head, and he shook his head, speechless.

"Kelly," he said, "you are a marvel."

We closed down our CarePages website and moved our progress reports to Facebook, inviting our friends to get back to a more normal method of communication. We thanked our CarePages community for all their support and prayers, knowing they had helped us get this far. I couldn't imagine what it would have been like going through that ordeal before the advent of e-mail and the Internet. Our ability to connect with friends and loved ones using technology, along with the resources available to us online, was truly a godsend.

The holidays were approaching, and little by little, I knew I was getting better.

Brad

You don't know what you're getting into until you're in the middle of it.

All the professionals challenged us, "The more work you put into it, the more you will get out of it and the faster you will improve." We were still working against the six-month deadline they had warned us about, while simultaneously making sure Kelly showed steady progress so that the insurance company would continue to approve therapy. We were learning how the health care system works as we went, and at times, it felt more difficult than Kelly's brain damage. There were two-week progress reports from therapy that had to be sent in detail back to Kelly's physical and mental rehabilitation (P&MR) doctor from the rehab facility. He then had to summarize her progress and send the report to the insurance company to approve a prescription for another four weeks of therapy. Every four weeks, we had to resubmit, and if any communication broke down or a form wasn't filled out correctly by a clerical person, therapy stopped. This happened to us a couple of times before we figured it out, and I would double- and triple-check with phone calls and e-mails to make sure the paperwork got processed. I felt like a failure when this breakdown happened, because Kelly was working her butt off, and I just needed to make sure the medical professionals and insurance company didn't slow her down.

The same type of process applied to all her medicines too, and there were a bunch. The most important were her antiseizure meds, but all of them had functions and different dosages and administration schedules. Eventually, I put all the information into a spreadsheet, so I wasn't relying on her or my memory. It was also interesting that many times we would have to remind the doctors what her regimen was. I get it—they are busy and have a ton of patients. Still, if they didn't have it down for sure, I knew we'd better take control.

Throughout the first few months of rehab, I felt as if I were stumbling around in the dark, looking for the light switch. If we had questions, we could usually find someone to answer them, but the problem was that we didn't even know which questions to ask until something caught us by surprise. We didn't know what we didn't know. I was still the quarterback of Team Kelly, but much of the time, I had no idea what plays to call.

According to the doctors, we had a finite time frame to make as much progress as possible to rebuild Kelly's body and mind, so other than my job, we put everything else on hold. Our social life vanished, and I stopped playing golf altogether and dropped our membership to our country club. This might not seem like a big deal, but I played golf in college, played a couple of times a week, and competed in tournaments locally, so a lot of our relationships and social time had been built around my golf and golfing buddies and their families. I was going to be spending most of my time at the rehab facility and getting all of our health care and financial affairs in order.

We developed a routine. In the morning, I checked in with work by phone and e-mail. Three days a week, I drove her to therapy. I sat in on the physical and occupational therapy, but she still didn't want me to attend her speech therapy, so I would camp out in the lunchroom with patients and staff and work by e-mail. However, I'd be there to help her if she had questions or wasn't able to articulate what she wanted to say. I observed her sessions carefully and asked questions about what exercises we could practice on our own.

Another tip I figured out along the way is that doctors and nurses are mostly tech-forward, and if you don't abuse the privilege, they are happy to give you their e-mail addresses, which they monitor constantly. Rather than wasting hours getting frustrated in calling through automated answering services at the hospitals and talking to clerical people, I could e-mail or text them and hear back in minutes or hours versus waiting and wondering if they ever got the message. This was particularly helpful with prescriptions, questions about ongoing symptoms, and insurance paperwork and protocols.

On the days Kelly didn't have therapy, I would help her exercise at home. We alternated routines, because the muscles, like anything, need time to recover. So on her off days, we worked together for a couple of hours each morning on strength and stretching exercises.

We worked on a lot of muscle-coordination activities, trying to relearn how to use her right arm and rebuild arm muscles that were atrophied. One exercise for her still-immobile right leg had her lie on the bed on her stomach, and I would tap the back of her leg to stimulate the muscle and help her lift her calf and foot up so that I could catch her foot with my hand. Over time, she needed me lifting less as she rebuilt her muscle memory, basically rewiring her circuitry through repetition.

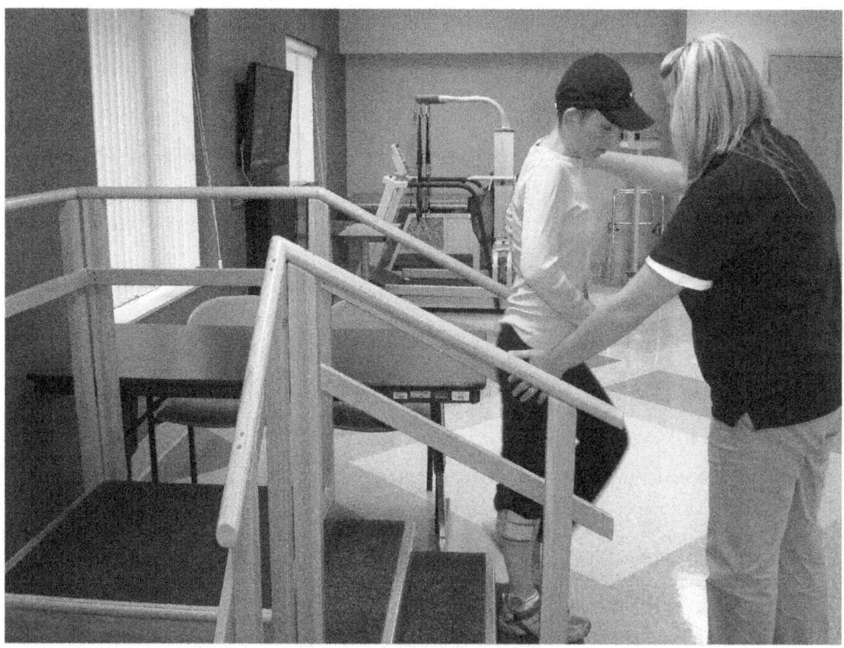

This work was a big part of Kelly's recovery. This is where many people don't have the support or will to put in the work at home, which dramatically affects their likelihood of a full recovery. In this department, Kelly excelled. She had established high goals for herself to get as close to

100 percent better as fast as she could. She was self-motivated; there was never a time when I had to force it and say, "No, we really have to do this."

Of course, there were parts of the regimen she liked better than others, and some activities were more frustrating than others. I'm sure there were days when she thought it was going to be easier or faster or felt sad or hopeless, but it hardly ever showed. She was courageous and tough.

She was my hero.

I came home one day and saw a "Never give up" plaque hanging in the kitchen. She was philosophical—more philosophical than the old Kelly. She often said, "Two steps forward and one back," but she kept stepping up and never gave up. I was glad to see that she was embracing what was ahead. That plaque remains in our office, where it inspires us every day.

Just When You Get Comfortable

One day in May, I was in a meeting at work, when my iPhone vibrated. Before the stroke, I never would have let a personal call or text interrupt a meeting. In fact, I prided myself on keeping my personal life separate from my work life.

That had all changed now. I took the call. It was Kelly, who was at home alone.

"Brad, I feel weird."

"What's wrong? What is it?" My adrenaline skyrocketed as I heard the panic in her voice.

"I don't know. I've been feeling weird since last night. Maybe it's allergies or a cold coming on, but it's just weird. Something's not right."

Her voice faded in and out, and her speech was shaky and slurred. I flashed back to the airport and the last time I'd been unable to understand what she was trying to tell me.

"Call 911," I said. "I'm getting in the car right now."

With apologies to my colleagues, I hightailed it out of the office, and a few minutes later, I was speeding down I-75 from Cincinnati into Kentucky. My phone rang again.

"Brad?" It was Kelly's sister, Katie.

Oh shit, I thought. "What? How is she? What's going on?"

"It's okay, Brad; don't panic. Kelly called me, and I called 911. A sheriff who lives in your neighborhood was there in no time. She's on her way to the hospital."

That was little comfort to me considering what had happened the last time Kelly went to the hospital in an ambulance.

This can't be happening again! I thought. *We've come so far.* All the worst possible thoughts and fears raced through my mind.

I practically flew to the hospital, the same one she had been admitted to that terrible day in August. I slammed the car into a parking spot and ran into the ER. It was only a matter of moments before a doctor was there to give me the news.

"She's going to be fine," he said, to my relief. "She experienced what's called a focal seizure, a seizure in one specific spot in her brain. It's focused so precisely that it might not seem like what you think of as a seizure. It was probably affecting just one part of her functioning and likely presented itself similar to her initial stroke symptoms. We've given her Ativan."

"Her speech did sound off when we were on the phone, but it couldn't have been a seizure," I protested. "She takes seizure medication every day."

"The seizure medication can limit seizures but not eliminate them entirely. She will be at risk for these focal seizures, probably for the rest of her life."

I asked him about the symptoms of a focal seizure so we'd know what to look out for in the future, and when he mentioned that slurred speech and weakness in her extremities were possibilities, I wondered why we hadn't already been told about this risk. When I got to see Kelly, she was still struggling to say her birthday and address, she had a bit of twitching in the right corner of her mouth, and her right eye was half shut. We learned that day that we shouldn't panic if it happens again, because it's not a stroke and cannot cause further damage. The brain gets distracted with the seizure and forgets all the things it has relearned, and the seizure shows up with some of the same physical and cognitive symptoms. We also learned that Ativan is a great emergency plan in case of seizure, as it will immediately knock the seizure out and let her rest.

The whole event was scary and served as an effective reminder that it was all up to us.

She had told me the day before that she was feeling a little weird and had some numbness, but she just thought she was tired or getting a cold. We know now that a focal seizure is sometimes preceded by signs and feelings called an aura, which can include sudden and inexplicable feelings of fear, anger, sadness, happiness, or nausea. There might be sensations of falling or movement; unusual feelings or sensations or an altered sense of sound, smell, taste, sight, and touch; or feelings that the environment is not real. Sometimes a sense of spatial distortion accompanies a focal seizure; things close by might appear to be at a distance, or the patient might feel a sense of déjà vu, have labored speech, or be unable to speak at all. Random focal seizures are not uncommon for stroke survivors as the brain continues to heal. It would have been great to know this before it happened to us. The scary thing is, the seizure can look a lot like the initial stroke if you don't know any better, which we didn't.

Fortunately, Kelly was able to go home that night, with a prescription for Ativan that we could keep on hand in case the symptoms recurred.

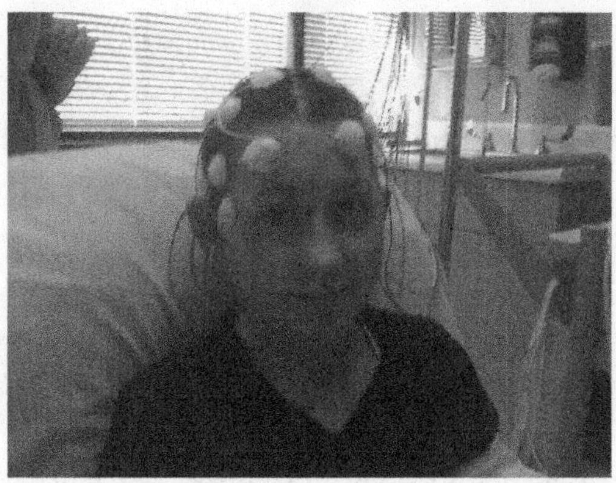

It was frustrating to once again face a situation that was unremarkable to the medical professionals but that had never been explained to us. However, we were learning to expect that and to deal with it.

If we had to be on our own, we were beginning to like our team's chances.

If We Only Knew: You Are in Charge

- Develop a one-arm wardrobe. It sucks, but if you've had a stroke, you need to overhaul your wardrobe if you want to be independent. That means no more heeled shoes, button-up tops, laced shoes, necklaces, bracelets, or tight jeans. It might not be forever, but T-shirts, sweats, and slip-on or Velcro gym shoes are the easiest.

- You probably won't be the same size due to swelling and the hospital diet and meds.

- Recognize the difficulty of a one-arm kitchen and laundry. If you need two hands to do a task, then you need an alternative plan. Sometimes adaptive tools can help, but in the beginning, it might be easier to hire someone or ask a family member to take care of these tasks so that you can focus on getting better.

- Keep records. You will need a binder, probably several. Over time, you will build in-depth records for therapy, medicine, health insurance, disability, social security, legal guardianship, and Medicare. These will all become sections of the binder.

- Be knowledgeable about the insurance process. Have your caregiver or helper call the insurance company to find out all the rules and reporting requirements so that you can stay on top of the medical and rehab staff and process. This can be an enormous amount of red tape. If therapist A doesn't fill out the form correctly, therapy can stop. Know what has to happen, write it down, and ensure the forms are completed correctly.

- Understand the prescription regimen. Your caregiver or helper should ask about and document what each medicine is designed to do and the long-term plan of attrition. Keep a spreadsheet if you have to, but have it readily available to give out to anyone who asks. You would think doctors know everything going on with prescriptions, but often, they don't. The information you have about the prescriptions can make a big difference.

- Make sure you have communication details. Get the names, e-mail addresses, and phone numbers of key people, and keep them in the file. As long as you don't abuse the privilege, you might be able to e-mail or text questions and get answers faster than if you were to call and leave a message.

- Be aware of seizure risk. Ask about the risk, and know the signs. Create a plan in case a seizure happens.

CHAPTER 10

Defining Our New Normal

Kelly

I had begun to think a lot about sex, not in an "I've gotta have it" way but more in a "That's something I need to do to be normal again" kind of way. Our sex life before the stroke was great, and I was beginning to realize I missed that intimacy. I needed to feel that connection again and to know that I was still desirable to my husband.

We had hinted at it a couple of times, but we were both probably a little gun-shy about talking about it, much less doing it. I didn't know for sure if I was ready, but I wanted to just rip off the Band-Aid.

With my mom gone on a well-deserved vacation, I knew Brad and I would have a lot of time together, just the two of us, for the first time since the stroke. So I did it.

"Brad, I think we should have sex."

His eyes widened. "No," he said, "I don't really think that's a good idea. Not yet."

"Yes, we need to do it. You won't break me," I said. The look in his eyes confirmed he was worried about what might happen. "You won't hurt me. I still can't feel a lot on my right. Let's try it. We have some lost time to make up for, so we can try it, and if it doesn't work, we'll just deal with that."

So we agreed to at least try. I won't lie—it was awkward and uncomfortable. With limited feeling on my right side, I needed to lift up my leg with my hand and move it to where it needed to be. We tried to relax, remember how we used to fit together, and adapt to my new limitations and Brad's caution.

Finally, we did it, or some version of it, and afterward, we cried and laughed and hugged.

I wouldn't trade that terrible attempt at sex for all the world. It was an expression of our continuing love for each other and a celebration of my ongoing recovery. It was an experience so intense and personal that crying was the only appropriate reaction. I felt that we were on our way, that we had reached another kind of milestone.

"We will always remember this—in a good way," I whispered to Brad. "We're going to be fine. And next time, we're going to do that better."

It did get better. But we needed to practice a lot.

A New Recruit to Team Kelly

As I got stronger in the year following the stroke, we were able to visit family for dinner and even go out to nearby restaurants. Each outing took some planning, and we would call ahead to be sure we knew if there were stairs or other obstacles that I would have to negotiate. Once we found a restaurant that worked well with my new restrictions, we tended to go back regularly.

My mom had returned to Florida, and Brad was back at work full-time, but I wasn't totally on my own. I had a steady stream of visitors to the house, and there was always someone calling to check on me.

It was frustrating to have to ask for any help at all. I had always been my own person, and I was angry to have had that taken away, but over time, I came to terms with it.

"I don't want to have this big, long list of things I can't do that you have to do," I told Brad finally. "That's not fair to you. I need some help."

"What kind of help?" he asked. "Should we call one of those home-care companies?"

"I don't want to do that," I said. "I want someone who will help me but not treat me like I am disabled."

In a stroke of luck, we found Sue from Best Friend Errand Service, a company that provides concierge service to help all kinds of people with their to-do lists. The two of us hit it off right off the bat. It wasn't long until we were like Lucy and Ethel, laughing our way through the aisles at Home Depot or in the waiting room at my doctor's appointments. By being more of a friend than an employee, she made it easier for me to accept the help I needed. She also took a load off Brad's mind.

Some chores that had been mine in my previous life had to be handled differently. I had always liked ironing, but I don't like it anymore, so I discovered the dry-cleaner delivery service, something I'd seen the neighbors use before but hadn't considered for myself. I did a lot of minor DIY maintenance at our old house, and I was always okay with that. I could do it on the weekends when Brad was golfing. But I can't do that anymore, so I found a handyman in case Brad isn't around or it's something he can't do or doesn't want to do.

I was still determined to do most of the shopping by myself, even though it was an effort to push the cart and avoid bumping into other carts, displays, or even kids. I needed to constantly scan left and right, looking to my blind spot.

As I made my way through the aisles, I was keenly aware of how I must have looked to other people. Were they staring? I couldn't tell. Surely they were looking longer than they should have. What were they thinking?

C'mon, Kelly, I thought to myself. *Why should you care what those people are thinking? You don't know them, and they don't know anything. Just ignore it.* But that was easier said than done.

It was almost easier when children pointed and asked, "Mommy, what's wrong with that lady?" This seemed to snap their parents out if it and make them realize how impolite it was to stare. They almost always shushed the offending toddlers and hustled them around the corner.

Sometimes a well-meaning adult would smile sympathetically, nod toward my WalkAide, and say, "Ski accident?" The old Kelly would have buried the feelings of anger that accompanied these inquiries, but the new filter-free me had a hard time with that.

"Stroke," I would say bluntly, stopping the conversation dead in its tracks. Somehow, the stricken looks on the faces of women my own age upon hearing that word made me feel better. That was a feeling I wasn't used to having.

The new Kelly *was* kind of a fitch, but I was starting to really like her.

Healing Is a Full-Time Job

As my therapy proceeded, the question of returning to work continued to nag at me. By now, I was beginning to remember the person I had been before and realize what I was lacking. When Father K or my other work friends came to visit, I would say, "I remember my job. I love that job. I need to get back to work."

I knew now what I was working toward slowly but surely.

At the beginning of November 2009, just more than two months after my stroke, I thought, *I need to do all this therapy so I can go back to work. I need to really focus on this, and in a month, I'll be fine.*

Then November came and went, and I thought, *Well, it's going to take a little longer, but I'm still working toward going back to work.*

As my brain continued to heal, I began to remember what my job entailed, and I could see how far I was from being able to perform at the level I had before. I had always been a speed reader; I'd been able to read a book in an hour and a half. I had been a good writer and a confident spokesperson for the college.

In early December, Brad took me to visit my office and see my colleagues. Everyone welcomed me with warmth and a few tears, and my office looked just as I had left it. The work had gone on in my absence, but my job, colleagues, and old life were all there waiting for me.

Still, I suspected that when people said, "We can't wait for you to come back!" they were probably thinking, *Oh my gosh, poor Kelly. She's not the same. She's never coming back*. Even so, they held my job for me while everyone chipped in to get my work done, and I continued to believe.

As the holidays approached, I told Brad, "I'm doing okay, but boy, I think it's going to take a little more time."

Most of the time, I could heed Brad's caution to take things one at a time, but one day, shortly before Christmas and after a particularly bad rehab session, I broke down. As always, Brad was there for me.

"It's been almost three months, Brad," I said through my sobs. "I am getting better. My speech is better, and I've come so far from where I started. But I can see it's going to take a lot more time. How can I possibly do that job again? I can't write, I can't speak well, and I can't even get through the day without lying down to rest. Maybe I'm not going to be able to go back to work after all."

Brad knew how much pride I took in my career and how much satisfaction it gave me. As long as he'd known me, my work and my family had been the things that defined me. It was much more than just a job.

"We don't have to decide anything right now," he said, trying to reassure me. "Let's just take it day by day. You're not getting any pressure from the college, and it's still early." He held me close and stroked my hair as my sobs subsided.

"No," I said. "No, I can't do it. It's too much. I just need to focus on one thing, my health. I think I need to resign."

Brad looked at me solemnly. "Are you sure that's what you want to do?" he asked.

"No, I don't want to do it," I said, correcting him. "I have to. I love my job, but there's no way I can be the person I used to be and do justice to the job, the people, and the college. I just can't."

"If that's your decision, I'll support you one hundred percent," Brad said.

Almost immediately, I felt a weight lift off my shoulders. The decision was one of the hardest I've ever had to make, but the feeling of relief that washed over me once I said it out loud proved to me that it was the right choice.

Now all I had to do was tell the college. Brad and I met for lunch with Cathy, my boss and close friend, over the holiday break. We were almost finished with lunch, when I said, "All right, Cath, I need to let you know that I'm going to resign."

"Oh, Kelly." Her voice caught in her throat, and her eyes welled with tears. "Are you sure? You don't have to. We can hold your job longer."

"No, I'm sure. Brad and I have given it a lot of thought, and I need to focus on my recovery. It may be a long time before I can work again. Maybe never. You need to have somebody in that position."

"I understand," she said. "Really, I do. But I don't have to like it."

So on a Friday afternoon in early January, just more than four months after my stroke, Brad took me to my office to box everything up. The office was nearly empty late on a Friday afternoon, as I knew it would be. I didn't want a scene or a big good-bye.

As we packed my files, photographs, and coffee mug, I repeated to myself, "New, fresh start. New year." I looked forward to wiping this slate clean and moving on. I was moving into the unknown, but that was okay, I told myself. That was a good thing.

I looked back at the building as we walked to the car. That was that. I was no longer a career woman. I silently vowed to renew my efforts at recovery. Just because I had quit this job didn't mean I would never have another one. I wanted to be able to say to everybody, "Ha, I did it. I can really bounce back."

"Wait a minute." I stopped and turned to Brad. "What about the money? Are we going to be okay without me working?" I hadn't even thought of that, but now that I had, I was concerned.

Brad said, "Don't worry. We'll be okay. That's the least of our worries."

Whether it was a worry or not, Brad was not going to put that on me. I think he knew long before I did that I wouldn't be going back to work, just as my colleagues probably knew.

I will be forever grateful that not a single one of them, including Cathy, told me that hard truth during those early months of struggle. I guess they could see how important it was for me to believe that I would make it back to the office.

Every once in a while, I still have a little twinge of something—not regret exactly but more like a sense of loss, a feeling that something is missing. But I don't regret my decision at all, and I don't look back. I believe that God has a plan for everything, even though sometimes I didn't like the way his plan was going.

Resigning from my job to focus on recovery was the first step toward acceptance of my new normal. I felt as if I were finally coming to terms with my situation, and I was ready to do that. I can't tell you why that was the point where I started getting comfortable with my new life and my limitations. I'm sure that point is different for everyone, but there will come a time when you have to forget about what happened, stop hanging on to the past, and focus on the future. For me, my faith in God helped me find my way, and my commitment to Brad to get better for him and us was what kept me motivated.

Things would never be the same as they had been, but I was closing the door to my past life and opening myself up to a new future, a new normal.

If We Only Knew: Coming to Terms

- Accept your new normal. Finding your source of motivation will be important to moving forward in your recovery, but it will take time. As the first few months go by at home, recognize that things will continue to change, and progress is not always linear. Some days will be better than others. Whatever your new ambition is, it will help you through your day-to-day limitations.

- Recognize that relationship challenges are normal. In addition to the physical limitations, there might be emotional challenges for a stroke survivor. A stroke doesn't just affect the survivor; it affects everyone around the survivor. Above all, remember to be patient with everything. For Brad and Kelly, reestablishing intimacy was important, but there might be other relationship issues to address. Keep the lines of communication open, and don't hesitate to seek counseling.

- Give the patient time. As a caregiver, you might realize early on the likely limitations the person will face, but you need to let the stroke survivor come to terms with it at his or her own pace. Positivity and encouragement are what is needed. That said, you must plan accordingly in terms of your finances and other household needs.

- Don't neglect caregivers' care. Initially, most caregivers don't mind giving 100 percent to allow a stroke survivor to recover, but as time goes on, the demands of working and taking on caregiving tasks can feel like too much. In the beginning, there might be a lot of offers for help. Accept them, because these offers can decrease as time goes on. Think about what you can delegate so that there isn't such a heavy load on the caregiver. Think about what you're going to need in the long term, and research how to get it. Caregiver support groups can help with this as well.

- Caregiver help is important. Brad and Kelly were lucky that Kelly's mother and Brad's brother were able to stay in their house during the first year so that Brad could travel for work. You can also search the web and find transportation services comfortable with limited-mobility customers, in-home trainers, and personal assistant services. These all exist in most areas, and expenses can qualify as health savings account expenses and be tax deductible.

- Explore financial resources. Talk to your health care providers about foundations and state and national funding sources. Many states have a traumatic brain injury fund, and stroke falls in that category. A list of some of Brad and Kelly's appears in the appendix.

CHAPTER 11

Mishaps and Milestones

Kelly

After the holidays, we turned the page from 2009 to 2010. We believed it would be a new year, and I was ready. Little did I know the challenges that lay ahead.

In January, I settled into my therapy with a new determination. Every two weeks, we sat down with the therapists to review what I had accomplished and set new benchmarks. The therapists sent the reports to my neurologist so that he could keep up with my progress, and Brad helped make sure the insurance approval process stayed on track.

While I was making great strides within the walls of therapy, applying my newly regained skills in the real world was a different story—and sometimes a funny one.

One day I decided to make lasagna for Brad. It was another step on the road to feeling normal—doing something as simple as making a meal I had cooked dozens of times before. I was looking forward to seeing his face when I presented him with this great meal I had prepared all on my own.

I sautéed onions and meat, boiled noodles, and grated cheese. Painstakingly, I layered the glass baking dish with the ingredients until I had a beautiful pan of lasagna. The task might have taken three hours instead of one, but I was proud I had done it all by myself.

"This is great," I said to myself as I opened the oven door. "You really did it, Kel."

But I spoke too soon. As I lifted the pan from the counter and turned toward the oven, I saw it begin to slip from my right arm. "No, no, no, no, no!" I shouted. "No!"

As if in slow motion, the pan slid down and crashed onto the open oven door. My carefully assembled masterpiece scattered across the kitchen floor as I looked on helplessly.

I couldn't grab with any of my fingers on that hand, so I had tried to balance the dish between my forearm and my body and had overestimated what my neglected right arm could support. I was devastated.

I collapsed to the floor amid the mozzarella and tomato sauce. "All I wanted to do was prepare one simple meal!" I howled at my useless right hand. "Is that so much to ask? Could you not just help me get one lousy pan of lasagna into the oven?"

"Kelly! What happened?"

I looked up to see Brad in the doorway. "Oh, Brad," I sobbed. "I just wanted to do something simple all by myself. And look! Look at the mess I made! I can't do anything."

"It's okay," he said. "Let's get you up out of this mess, and we'll clean it up."

"Today was not a good day. I just need to go to bed." I knew that with a good night's sleep, I could begin again, refreshed and recommitted. I channeled Scarlett O'Hara with my new mantra: "Tomorrow is another day."

As a young stroke survivor, you will also have days when the simplest things give you trouble, and depending on where your stroke was, your challenges might be different from mine. Learning to handle the frustration as you move forward in recovering is an important skill. For me, getting a good night's sleep and putting the struggle behind me was important, but others might find that talking with therapists or trying different activities are more effective. In any case, dwelling on failure will stop your recovery faster than anything, because you must try and fail in order to relearn how to do things.

Going Out: A Whole Other Ball Game

Things sometimes got messy in the private arena of our own home, but going out in public sometimes meant even bigger hurdles. It was one thing to manage a trip to Walgreens on my own, but it would be another thing entirely to try to have the kind of active social life I was used to.

For instance, we love college basketball. It had always been one of our things, and floor-level seats are not easy to come by, so when Brad and a friend won four floor-level tickets to a University of Cincinnati basketball game, I knew how much he wanted to go with me. I wanted to go too, but it would not be easy.

Dinner conversation with the other couple that night included discussions of what we could do to minimize inconveniences. We tried to act as if it were just another night out with good friends, but of course, it wasn't. It was the new normal, the one that had us scrutinizing every step of the itinerary before we could relax and root for the Bearcats.

My main concern was the steeply stacked stairs around the arena that would take us down to our seats. I couldn't, and still can't, feel people on my right side, and there was no railing to hold on to. Brad stuck like glue to my left side, wrapping his right arm tightly around my waist, nearly lifting me off the bleacher steps.

Right foot down. Pause. Left foot down to meet it on that step. Repeat. One by one, we made our way down the flight of stairs to our seats, oblivious to the hoopla around us and impatient fans behind us.

When our feet finally hit the hardwood, it was all worth it. The basketball arena was familiar, and it felt normal to be there—not new normal, just normal. When a ball bounced off the court and hit Brad, I rolled it back inbounds to the referee as any other person would have.

"Did you see that, Brad?" I smiled. As always, I was glad we had powered through the tough part to get to the good part.

I can't remember whether UC won or lost that night, but getting through that outing without any major issues—and being able to relax and enjoy myself in the company of friends and fellow fans—was certainly a victory for me.

Up, Up, and Away

That winter, I was desperate to see some sunshine and get away from the cold and anxious to see my parents, who had left Cincinnati for their annual retreat to Florida. Brad had his annual sales meetings in New Orleans, so we planned that he would fly with me to Florida, spend a few days there with my parents, and then continue on to his meeting and come back to get me afterward.

"Brad, do you really think I can do it?" I asked. This would be my first time out of Cincinnati since the stroke, as well as my first flight and my first time away from home.

"Well," he said, "I know you'll be fine once we get there, but what do you think about the trip? How can we manage that?"

"I don't want to take a wheelchair to the gate. I want to walk."

He looked at me apprehensively. "That might be a long walk," he replied. "Are you sure?"

"Yes, I really want to go. Let's just do it."

We made the arrangements, and Brad helped me pack my bag. The morning of our departure, my stomach churned as we arrived at the airport. "I guess I'm a little more nervous than I thought I'd be," I said.

Ever the calming presence, Brad took my hand and murmured, "You've never loved flying, but it's going to be fine. I'm here. You can do this."

Our first obstacle was security, where the security personnel were unfamiliar with my WalkAide. I ended up having to walk through the x-ray machine without it.

Then we made our way to the escalator—an issue I hadn't even thought about. Suddenly, I was terrified. Moving stairs were even more intimidating than the steep bleachers at the arena. What if I got caught and fell or dragged a foot and tripped? Just like when I was a kid, I held my breath in anticipation of the dismount at the bottom.

As we headed toward our gate, Brad walked on my left side, so I could hold his hand where I'm strong and solid.

"I wish you'd let me walk on your right side to protect it," Brad said.

I knew it was probably better for him to guard my right side against the hurried and sometimes rude crowd, but I told him, "I like you better where I can feel you and see you. You'll just have to steer me away from people."

We moved out of the train, up the escalator, and down to our gate, which was at the farthest end of the concourse, of course. "I feel like we've run a marathon," I joked as we fell into our seats. "But we did it!" When we touched down in Florida two hours later and nothing bad had happened, I felt relieved.

I had checked another first off my list. I could travel again.

Going the Distance

Early in my therapy, toward the end of 2009, we had heard about the 1K Step for Stroke, a new addition to the Heart Association's spring event scheduled for March 2010. My neurologist was to be the master of ceremonies presiding over a thousand-kilometer walk of stroke survivors.

Finally, I had something to focus on other than my recovery. We were in. I stepped up my therapy to be sure I could endure to walk a kilometer through the downtown streets.

I could remember the days when I'd walked a kilometer in the house before breakfast.

We sent an e-mail out to friends, family, and colleagues, and as they always did, Team Kelly stepped up. By the day of the walk, we had raised $5,000 in contributions, and I reveled in the familiar feeling of doing something for others again.

The day of the walk, the weather was rough—as cold, wet, and windy as springtime in Ohio can be. My brother had entered the accompanying five-thousand-kilometer run, and my whole family had come downtown to cheer both of us on. I was just hoping I'd finish.

The crowd wasn't big, but that didn't matter to us—we all had our own reasons for being there. Cold weather is especially hard on people with nerve and brain damage, tightening up our weaker side to further challenge our movements. We hadn't considered Mother Nature when planning for this day, but I was determined, as were my fellow participants.

With an announcement and a flourish, the inaugural Steps for Stroke began.

Brad was at my side, holding my hand as we left the starting line. We made it one block with no problem and then another. Cameras clicked as family members walked alongside us, capturing the moment. We reached the halfway point and turned back for the finish line.

The empty city blocks looked endless.

"Brad, that looks much farther than I thought!" I exclaimed.

"I know. Look how far you've already walked," he said. "How are you feeling?"

"I feel good," I said. "I can see the finish line, and look—I'm in first place. Not that it's a race or anything. But still."

Brad laughed that my competitive streak was alive and well. "Let's keep it going then. Let's win this thing."

As we crossed the finish line, Brad and I kissed, our eyes welling up with a sense of accomplishment, celebration, pride, and loss. For the first time since the stroke, I had done something for a larger cause, and at the same time, I'd pushed myself to my physical limits. It wasn't the marathon I had once dreamed of running, but it was a special moment less than six months after I had awakened from my coma.

"I guess the first six months are the most important," I said to Brad.

"I guess so," he said. "And you kicked ass."

Pass or Fail

I might have conquered the first six months physically, but mentally, I still hadn't grasped my cognitive limitations. That became clear in my first meeting with a neuropsychologist.

No one suggested the meeting with the neuropsychologist until we were well into my recovery therapy, when I needed the evaluation to prove to the government that I was disabled. A neuropsychologist evaluates how the brain interacts with a person's behavior and cognitive capabilities. An evaluation includes tests for analytic and arithmetic logic and skills.

My first meeting was a four-hour neuropsychological evaluation, which included long interviews with a neuropsychologist and an alphabet soup of tests: the Test of Premorbid Functioning (TOPF), Wechsler Adult Intelligence Scale-IV (WAIS-IV), Kaufman Brief Intelligence Test-2 (KBIT-2), Delis-Kaplan Executive Function System (D-KEFS), Beck Depression Inventory II (BDI-II), and Personality Assessment Inventory (PAI), among others. The purpose of the tests was to ascertain where my deficits were and determine what I could work on. They were also used to show the government that I was disabled and could not work.

This was torture for me. I had always been an above-average student; I'd never struggled with learning, attention problems, or test anxiety. I graduated college with honors, and I had always scored well on standardized tests. I retained a self-image of a smart, capable person in every area of my life. But this was something else entirely.

Brad could not be with me for the testing, and I realized how much I counted on him in day-to-day situations to accommodate me and fill in the blanks. It was cognitive overload for me, turning my brain to mush and my self-confidence to doubt.

As the testing proceeded over several sessions, I knew I wasn't doing well, at least not according to my standards. I found myself making excuses for my performance: "I'm nervous" or "I've never been very good with directions." However, the doctor wasn't buying it—I could tell. There was more than one tearful episode as I powered through the sessions as best as I could.

I had been feeling good about my progress in every area, but these tests illustrated with perfect clarity how much I had lost. When we got the report, there it was in black and white.

Scale	Percentile Rank	Qualitative Description
Verbal Comprehension	16	Low Average
Perceptual Reasoning	39	Average
Working Memory	2	Extremely Low
Processing Speed	10	Low Average
Full Scale	9	Low Average

On test after test, scale after scale, the words flew off the page at me: *average, low average, borderline, extremely low,* and even *severe.* The extent of my deficits made a mockery of my Little Mary Sunshine "I'm at 75 to 80 percent of my prestroke capability" rating. What had I been thinking? I had been measuring myself against the bottom of the scale, my abilities when I awoke from the stroke, rather than the top of the scale, my prestroke abilities. Now these professionals were pointing out the obvious to me, which I didn't want to acknowledge.

I think if I went back and did these tests again, I would show off-the-charts improvement. I wouldn't be as good as I was prestroke—I mean, I was a CMO—but at the time, I worried that I would be stuck forever at low-average performance levels. It was a blow to the ego for sure. The awesome thing is that you can get better in terms of cognitive and communication abilities forever. There will be things I will never do again physically, but I can always learn new words and find new ways to improve my mind and how I use it in my daily activities. Especially for young people, this is an important insight. These abilities are much more in your control, when so much else requires other people's help.

Though I am not sure why the neuropsychological evaluation was delayed, there are other tests to consider. In my case, no one tested my eyes or my hearing, and we didn't think about it, perhaps assuming the doctors or physical therapist had done this already. When things have settled down a little bit after your release, consider going to an eye doctor and an ENT to have full evaluations on these senses. Consider asking for the neuropsychological evaluation quickly as well. Having specific information delivered from a specialist and not just a general examination can identify any deficits from the stroke and can help you form a targeted therapy program early.

Establishing Boundaries

After the assessment, I saw a therapist by myself, just twice. He was looking for signs that I was depressed or having trouble coping psychologically with the effects of the stroke. Ever the optimist, I started out by telling him I was fine, and mostly, I *was* fine. "I always say, 'It is what it is.' That's my new motto," I told him. "Every day is a different day, good or bad. But it gets better. It always gets better."

He continued to probe for problem areas, egging me on a little bit. Finally, I said, "Well, there is one thing that I need to be okay with, and I'm not there yet. It's my family."

I was surprised at the emotions that came with this release. "I love my family so much. We are so close. But as a group, they are just overwhelming for me now. How can I tell them that I'm the same but am different right now?"

"Different how?" he asked.

"I feel normal but altered a little bit, in a good way. One, I can't carry the burden of all the family stuff that I used to do. I'm not sorry that I helped care for my grandparents, but it's a different time for me now. I can't be the one who takes care of everyone else.

"Now I think there are three categories of activities for me. First, there are things that I love to do that I can still do. Then there are things I can't do, even if I want to. And third, there are some things I just don't want to do. Some of those are things that I used to want to do, but some of them are things I've never wanted to do and just did to make other people happy. I've always had a sense that supporting my family was my purpose. I've always helped all of them—my grandparents, my siblings, everyone. That was my role. That was my job in the family. And I think I was good at it."

The therapist nodded his understanding. "It's perfectly reasonable for you to feel that way. You are not the person, physically or emotionally, that you were before. They need to understand that. What else would you like to say to them?"

I thought for a minute. "Sometimes, when I'm with them in a big group, I feel like I'm in a bubble."

"What do you mean a 'bubble'?" he asked.

I explained to him my theory of invisibility.

"How does that make you feel?" he said.

"Like I'm not even there. Or like they think I'm a baby or an idiot. Sometimes when I'm talking, they will just turn away from me and start talking to someone else. Brad will even say, 'Hey, do you realize Kelly's not finished with what she was saying?' I guess they've always been like that. I was probably like that too before. But I can't hold my own in those conversations anymore. I'm not quick enough to stand up for myself or to get my two cents in."

"Have you tried just saying that to them? Just asking them to be aware of that?"

"No, I haven't."

"Do you think you can be honest with your family and have that conversation now?"

"Yes," I said, surprising myself. "I can. I have to."

He had given me the validation and the permission I needed to focus on myself. That night, I talked to Brad. "I just need to figure out what I'm going to do. I have to tell people that I love them and that they helped me a lot, but I can't go back to certain things. I think they're all expecting that at a certain point, I'm going to be back to the Kelly who always took care of everybody. But I just can't do that anymore. I have to put myself first now."

"You have to tell them, Kelly," Brad said.

"I know I do," I said.

Eventually, I found ways to tell them about my new reality—my mom, dad, and whole family. I worked it into conversations on the phone or in person as casually as I could.

It usually sounded something like the following: "This is the deal, you guys. I've done a lot for family and friends over the years. I've helped you with your work and your schoolwork. I still love you all so much, and I'm so grateful for your love and support. But I am just going to have to be more careful about the obligations I take on. I won't be able to come to every family event.

"Also, I'm asking you to please not talk to other people about me. If you're upset about something that has to do with me, call me. Don't talk to each other about it. And try to be patient with me. I may not seem like it, but I'm following the conversations, and I want to participate. It just takes me a few seconds to collect my thoughts and process my words."

Their initial reactions were a mixture of surprise and confusion. They weren't used to hearing things like that from me. However, as they began to understand what I was saying, they accepted it matter-of-factly.

Everyone seemed to understand and promised to try to be more patient and understanding.

"That almost seemed too easy. I guess I was expecting some pushback, but they all seemed fine," I told Brad.

"It's like when you were in the hospital and the nurses told us the commotion was overwhelming for you. We just didn't know, and once we did, we all tried to act differently," Brad said.

In spite of my skepticism, neuropsychological therapy had turned out to be a good thing for me.

If We Only Knew: Setting Goals Is Tough

- Small wins add up. You have to set goals in rehab and therapy that are attainable. It takes time, but small wins add up. Things like climbing a step, kicking a ball, and saying and writing a word are big small wins. I set weekly goals for myself that went beyond my therapy goals. Speech, occupational, and physical therapy all translated to things at home I had to relearn, and I wrote them all down in my goals book and checked them off as I relearned how to do everyday activities and increase my vocabulary. You might have other small real-life goals. Try to achieve them while remembering that it can take time and patience to do so.

- Seek out specialist testing. For whatever reason, no one recommended we see a neuropsychologist until well into outpatient therapy, so we didn't know the full extent of cognitive damage, nor did anyone test Kelly's sight or hearing, as an eye doctor or ENT specialist would. Our advice would be to push for these assessments early so that you can understand the full extent of any damage that might not be visible to the naked eye. Don't assume the tests have been done.

- The neuropsychology evaluation is an important step in understanding long-term cognitive capabilities, including analytic and arithmetic logic and skills. The results will likely be demotivating at first, but they are important in helping the patient and caregiver face the reality of what has happened. The doctor will also assess the patient's overall attitude, state of depression or grief, and likely future mental capacity and outlook. On a practical note, the assessment will be required when you apply for short- and long-term disability benefits.

- Setting limits is important. As you come to know the new person you've become after a stroke, don't be afraid to ask for counseling if you need it. It's a huge emotional shift to need to recover, and needing help is normal. It's also normal to set limits in your relationships. There are some things you cannot do, but there are also some things you might not want to do. Communicate these limits kindly, and seek the advice of a therapist if you need help doing so.

CHAPTER 12

A New Start

Kelly

With the six-month window closing, the outpatient rehab facility I'd been attending had exhausted their resources, and we had reached the end of that road.

"I just don't see the point in continuing with therapy there," I said to Brad in despair. "They said I can keep going, but we'll just be doing the same things I'm already doing at home. There must be something else."

While I had blown away many expectations in my first six months, I still was nowhere near where I wanted to be and not ready to stop rehab just because they'd run out of new challenges for me.

By this time, Brad and I were turning into professional Googlers. We both spent hours surfing the Internet for information on stroke recovery. I'd joined an online forum of young stroke survivors. For the first time, I really felt that I wasn't alone in this. Other young people suffered strokes and recovered. I was buying books online, even though I couldn't read them. Brad would read sections to me, but the books piled up on my bedside table as a constant reminder that I wanted to learn to read again and be better.

When you are a younger stroke survivor and hungry for new ways to improve your quality of life, you have to do the homework. Solutions don't fall out of the sky. Of course, we say this now in hindsight, but we expected all those more knowledgeable than us to help us. That just doesn't happen. We have shared some websites and books we found through our own efforts at the end of this book, but a lot will depend on where you live and the care available in that area, as well as your insurance and financial options.

About the time we felt we were hitting a dead end, I had my regular appointment with the seizure specialist for my six-month EEG. When I mentioned my situation with the outpatient therapy, he said, "You know, your inpatient rehab facility up in Cincinnati has a program called the START program. It stands for Stroke Team Assessment and Recovery Treatment. It's a new approach for patients who are at least six months poststroke. They're doing some really innovative work that shows patients can continue to regain function after that traditional six-month window. I think you should check it out."

The minute we got home from the seizure specialist's office, we beelined for the computer to research the START program. It was an innovative program that used a team of seven specialists to assess stroke survivors and develop an individualized plan. We were shocked to find that the lead doctors in the program were my doctors, the ones we had been seeing regularly since my discharge from the inpatient facility.

That night, we fired off e-mails to all our doctors at that facility, asking about the program and whether I would qualify for it. The responses came quickly.

"Yes, I think you'd be a good candidate for this program. I don't know why we didn't recommend it to you," said one doctor.

My neurologist said, "I'm so sorry. I should have thought about you for the START program."

In late May 2010, I applied for admission to the program, submitting a full patient history and progress reports from my outpatient rehab and from my doctors. I was accepted into the program, and on June 22, I underwent a complete assessment to plan my rehabilitation program.

The assessment included my own evaluation of my mobility, my independence, and the impact the stroke had had on my life, as well as a physical assessment by the program's therapists. (See appendix A.) There was also a psychological component of the assessment, which evaluated both me and Brad for signs of depression.

The final question asked me to rate my recovery on a scale of 0 to 100, with 100 being full recovery. I rated myself at 75 to 80. Looking back now, that number strikes me as almost ridiculously optimistic. I was nowhere near 80 percent of my former self, but seeing the glass half full was what was keeping me going.

REHABILITATION SCREEN

System	Sign or Symptom	No	Yes (explain the problem)
1. Communication	Difficulty speaking, finding words or being understood, mumbling, slurring	NO	
2. Swallowing	Difficulty eating, drinking, or chewing, choking, coughing or gagging, drooling, feeling as if food is caught in mouth or throat	NO	
3. Voice	Change in loudness or tone of voice, hoarseness	NO	
4. Ears	Difficulty hearing	NO	
5. Thinking Skills (Cognition)	Difficulty with memory, attention, planning, problem solving, and organizing your thoughts.	NO	
6. Activities of Daily Living	Difficulty with bathing, grooming, feeding, toileting, uses adaptive equipment to complete tasks	NO	
7. Home Management	Difficulty with cooking, cleaning, bills, living independently	NO	[illegible] Dinner
8. Hand Splint	Do you currently wear a hand splint on your affected arm?	NO	
9. Exercise/ Workout	Difficulty doing an exercise program for your arm and/or leg?	NO	
10. Transfers	Difficulty with standing up, getting into bed, getting on/off the toilet, getting in/out of the car	N	
11. Balance	Have you fallen in the past year?		yes- January 2015
12. Walking	Difficulty walking by yourself?	NO	Does someone provide assistance? Do you use a cane/walker? How far can you go?
13. Orthotic/Brace	Do you currently wear a leg brace on your affected leg?	NO	yes- Walkaid
14. Wheelchair	Do you currently rely on a wheelchair for mobility in the house and community?	NO	How old is your wheelchair?
15. Recreation/ Quality of Life	Do have concerns about how your stroke has affected you socially with leisure activities? Hobbies?	NO	

Nine Symptom Checklist

Patient Name Kelly Marsh DOB 3-5-73

Appointment Date June 22, 2010

Over the last 2 weeks, how often have you been bothered by any of the following problems?

1. Little interest or pleasure in doing things
   ✓ not at all (0) ___ several days (1) ___ more than half the days (2) ___ nearly every day (3)
2. Feeling down, depressed or hopeless
   ✓ not at all (0) ___ several days (1) ___ more than half the days (2) ___ nearly every day (3)
3. Trouble falling or staying asleep or sleeping too much
   ✓ not at all (0) ✓ several days (1) ___ more than half the days (2) ___ nearly every day (3)
4. Feeling tired or having little energy
   ✓ not at all (0) ___ several days (1) ___ more than half the days (2) ___ nearly every day (3)
5. Poor appetite or overeating
   ___ not at all (0) ___ several days (1) ✓ more than half the days (2) ___ nearly every day (3)
6. Feeling bad about yourself or feeling that you are a failure or have left yourself or your family down
   ___ not at all (0) ✓ several days (1) ___ more than half the days (2) ___ nearly every day (3)
7. Trouble concentrating on things such as reading the newspaper or watching television
   ___ not at all (0) ___ several days (1) ✓ more than half the days (2) ___ nearly every day (3)
8. Moving or speaking so slowly that other people could have noticed or the opposite – being so fidgety or restless that you have been moving around a lot more than usual
   ___ not at all (0) ✓ several days (1) ___ more than half the days (2) ___ nearly every day (3)
9. Thoughts that you would be better off dead or hurting yourself in some way
   ✓ not at all (0) ___ several days (1) ___ more than half the days (2) ___ nearly every day (3)

TOTAL SCORE: 6

If you have checked off ANY problems, how difficult have these problems made it for you to do your work, take care of things at home or get along with other people?

___ Not difficult at all ✓ Somewhat difficult ___ Very difficult ___ Extremely difficult

This questionnaire was developed by Dr. Robert L. Spitzer, Janet B. W. Williams, Kurt Kroenke and colleagues. Reproduced with permission of Dr. Spitzer for use in clinical practice. Copyright held by Pfizer Inc.

Our meetings with the doctors that day left us hopeful. "We're not promising miracles or a complete recovery," the codirector of the center told us. "What we are promising is to go beyond the standard treatment, to take a fresh look using a collaborative team approach. With your approval, we will test the newest treatments and tools to help you get the fullest recovery possible."

"Yes," his codirector added. "People used to think the three- or six-month window was a hard and fast rule. But we are seeing that with these intensive treatments, people can have motor and cognitive recovery even several years later. If you are willing to work hard, we expect that you will continue to show improvement."

These words were music to my ears. God and everybody else knew by now that I could work hard. To think that I had some control over the outcome and that my progress wasn't doomed to stall after some arbitrary window had closed was all the motivation I needed.

A Look through Brad's Eyes

Included in the process was a caregiver self-assessment form intended to assess the state of mind of my primary caregiver. This evaluation was the first time I really understood Brad's perspective on our journey.

From the first day I became aware of my situation, I had worried about Brad. He had been the perfect caregiver in the hospital, in rehab, and now at home. He helped me in every way possible physically and mentally, not to mention all the doctor and insurance conversations. He even became my legal guardian so that he could speak for me in a legal sense, and we both had to go to court to prove that he wasn't stealing from me while he was helping me. We had to laugh at the process that made us prove he was only helping me as my guardian and not taking advantage of the situation. It was an odd relationship-building opportunity for both of us early in our marriage. He had been nothing but kind, patient, and supportive, but I still worried about how he must be feeling on the inside. Many times in these situations, particularly when the caregiver is a man, cracks can develop in a relationship or a life under the stress of supporting a stroke victim.

Seeing his responses to this assessment and realizing that he actually thought his life was better than it had been before my stroke blew me away. I always knew he was amazing, but this experience took that amazingness to a whole new level. I felt like the luckiest girl in the world.

BAKAS CAREGIVING OUTCOMES SCALE

Patient Name Kelly Marsh DOB 3/5/73

Caregiver's Name Brad Marsh Appointment Date 6/22/10

This group of questions is about the possible changes in your life from providing care for the stroke survivor. For each possible change listed, circle one number indicating the degree of change. The numbers indicating the degree of change range from -3 "Changed for the Worst" to +3 "Changed for the Best". The number 0 indicates "Did Not Change".

AS RESULT OF PROVIDING CARE FOR THE STROKE SURVIVOR:	Changed for the Worst			No Change	Changed for the Best		
1. My self esteem	-3	-2	-1	0	+1	+2	+3
2. My physical health	-3	-2	-1	0	+1	+2	+3
3. My time for family activities	-3	-2	-1	0	+1	+2	+3
4. My ability to cope with stress	-3	-2	-1	0	+1	+2	+3
5. My relationship w/ friends	-3	-2	-1	0	+1	+2	+3
6. My future outlook	-3	-2	-1	0	+1	+2	+3
7. My level of energy	-3	-2	-1	0	+1	+2	+3
8. My emotional well being	-3	-2	-1	0	+1	+2	+3
9. My roles in life	-3	-2	-1	0	+1	+2	+3
10. My time for social activities with friends	-3	-2	-1	0	+1	+2	+3
11. My relationship with family	-3	-2	-1	0	+1	+2	+3
12. My financial well being	-3	-2	-1	0	+1	+2	+3
13. My relationship with the stroke survivor	-3	-2	-1	0	+1	+2	+3
14. My physical functioning	-3	-2	-1	0	+1	+2	+3
15. My general health	-3	-2	-1	0	+1	+2	+3
16. In general, how has your life changed as a result of taking care of the stroke survivor	-3	-2	-1	0	+1	+2	+3

IF THERE ARE ANY OTHER CHANGES IN YOUR LIFE AS A RESULT OF PROVIDING CARE FOR THE STROKE SURVIVOR, PLEASE WRITE THE BELOW & RATE THEM ACCORDINGLY.

	Changed for the Worst			No Change	Changed for the Best		
17.	-3	-2	-1	0	+1	+2	+3
18.	-3	-2	-1	0	+1	+2	+3
19.	-3	-2	-1	0	+1	+2	+3

We received a summary of my START assessment along with a list of goals and a plan to achieve those goals. Every two weeks, my entire neurology and therapy team would reassess my progress against those goals and discuss my long-term plan. I was thrilled to see the extensive, detailed plan and fired up about getting started.

Dear **Ms. Marsh:**

Thank you for coming to the Stroke Recovery Center at Drake Center on **6/22/09**. Our multidisciplinary team comprehensively evaluates stroke recovery across multiple domains such as motor deficits and cognitive changes. Based on our assessments and our discussion with you, the following domains in your stroke recovery were identified:

ASSESSMENT

1) Motor Deficits- **You have some residual right sided weakness from your stroke. You have difficulty with walking due to weakness in your ankle and some spasticity in your right leg. Balance testing suggested that you are at a low risk for falls.**
2) Sensory Deficits- **You have a subjective 25-50% sensory deficit throughout your right side as a result of stroke.**
3) Speech- **You have difficulty with expressive language function, including word finding problems and occasional errors/substitutions. Your receptive function appears normal. You are relatively well compensated due to your high pre-stroke ability.**
4) Cognitive- **Cognitive testing showed a score of 23/30 (with 26/30 being normal). You struggled with complex tasks. You have recently seen a neuropsychologist at HealthSouth.**
5) Vision- **A right inferior visual field cut was noted.**
6) Emotional/Psychological- **The PHQ-9 score was 7. This suggests that you do not have active depression and/or anxiety at this time. You are currently taking Celexa. You may have had some anxiety issues and some obsessive/compulsive behaviors that have been less noticeable since the stroke.**
7) Symptomatic management- **You have spasticity in your right upper extremity, and had botox for your right lower extremity 1 month ago. You have seizures that are successfully managed with Keppra. You take Trazadone for sleep.**
8) Caregiver support/stroke education- **Your husband is an excellent provider. You are a good team who are very knowledgeable about stroke and aggressive in seeking care for recovery. Your husband is at some risk for caregiver burnout due to stress at work while he is simultaneously worrying about you. There seems to be some stress between your family and your husband.**
9) Medications and Stroke prevention- **You are not currently taking any medications for stroke prevention at this time.**
10) Wellness- **You have a reasonably high level of physical activity and you are working hard to improve your neurologic function.**

GOALS:

Based on our assessments and our discussions with you, we are establishing the following goals:

1.) **Improve language function.**
2.) **Improve leg/walking function.**
3.) **Improve fine motor control in right upper extremity.**
4.) **Return to driving.**

Based upon our assessment, in combination with your goals for stroke recovery, we recommend the following:

PLAN

1) Physical Therapy: **Refer for further therapy to improve function and endurance, and to enhance your exercise and stretching program. We will expand your current training program to include more balance activities and use of Walk Aide which has worked to break you out of the stiff knee pattern. Can continue to use cyclic functional e-stim. May include work in the pool as well.**
2) Occupational Therapy: **Refer for further therapy to improve upper extremity function and endurance, and to enhance your exercise and stretching program. Repeat driver testing. Will include forced use/constraint induced therapy. We will provide a resting splint. Will try sensory re-education.**
3) Speech/Language Pathology: **Referral for further therapy to improve high-level language function including outside activities; consider working with InReturn or other vocational type activities in short term.**
4) Cognitive: **We will continue to evaluate your cognitive function while in therapy. We would like to obtain any neuropsychometric testing results that you have already completed.**
5) Emotional/Psychological: **There is no evidence of depression and/or anxiety at this time. Continue to take Celexa at the present dose and we will continue to monitor for symptoms. You are planning to start psychotherapy both as a couple and individually based upon your previous evaluation at HealthSouth.**
6) Research: **You are a candidate for the L300 study but you are not interested because of the control group in the study that only recieves an AFO and you do not want to wear an AFO. You also are a candidate for our upper extremity mental practice study, will start this while beginning driver evaluation (i.e. before formal OT described above). You may also consider an aphasia study with Dr. Szaflarski, such as constraint induced language therapy.**
7) Symptomatic management: **You should continue to receive botox as needed for spasticity. Continue Keppra for seizures. Consider discontinuing trazadone?**
8) Caregiver: **Your husband should keep up the good work as your advocate, and continue to help you as needed although you are largely independent. Watch for signs of caregiver stress and burnout. Proceed with psychotherapy as mentioned above.**
9) Medications and Stroke Prevention: **Continue current regimen without change, except to add an enteric coated aspirin daily for stroke and cardiac event prevention. You should follow up with PCP to follow for risk factor monitoring.**
10) Wellness: **Continue to stay active and increase activity as tolerated. Consider taking on some new challenges, including short term vocational work (InReturn) or the challenge of starting and maintaining a young stroke support group.**

We will review your progress in **12-16 weeks**. Thereafter, we will determine when you should return to clinic. If you have any questions, please do not hesitate to contact us by phone or email.

Sincerely,

The Stroke Recovery Team at Drake.

Second Wind

Together with my new START team, I set goals for one month, two months, three months, four months, and a year. This was right up my alley.

They had much more technological equipment. They had a simulated car so that I could at least think about taking steps toward driving. There was a pool in which I could walk, and there were new and interesting ways to improve my balance and to master stairs. To address my right-side visual field cuts, I used a board on which I had to try to follow the light where numbers lit up. The purpose was to retrain my eyes to constantly scan to try to see everything.

"We'll never run out of things for you to do here, Kelly," one of the therapists told me. "You can do more and more. We can find other things for you to do."

Almost as important as the therapy, at least to me, was that I was surrounded by other patients. I enjoyed the camaraderie and fellowship of others in the same boat, talking to them before or after my sessions. The Young Stroke Survivor website and other online resources had been helpful, but I feel more connected when I can see people face-to-face.

Occasionally, the therapists would ask me to talk to another young stroke survivor who was early on in his or her recovery or to the parents or spouses to pass along some of my experiences and provide a positive example. When a new patient appeared in the START therapy room, I'd introduce myself right away. "What are you in for?" I'd say, which usually at least got me a smile.

Starting the program also felt a bit like coming home. This was the place where I had awakened from my month-long sleep, first understood what had happened to me, and taken my early steps to recovery. I was comfortable there and happy to have found more work to do.

The best part for Brad was that we got an actual caseworker, the quarterback he had been waiting for. Finally, there was someone other than us whose job was to coordinate my recovery plan, someone who actually knew the ins and outs of the medical system and could serve as my go-between and advocate with the therapists.

A larger facility meant more therapists and more flexibility in scheduling, but it also meant more red tape and communication issues. A few times, just when I was beginning to build a relationship with somebody, he or she would go on vacation without notice, and I'd have a different therapist who didn't know me or where I was in my recovery, which could set me off.

My speech was still the area where I was least satisfied with my progress, but I loved my new speech therapist.

"I love, or used to love, reading," I told her one day. "I want to try to read a book."

"Maybe we should just start with magazines," she said, bringing me back down to earth a bit. "Let's try this. Read one short article, and then write a little bit about it. Like a book report. How does that sound?"

"Yes!" I exclaimed. "That's a great idea!"

I started with half a page and then a page. I would write my report out by hand and then put it on the computer. For hours every day, I focused on my reading and writing; it felt like being back in college. If I didn't remember or didn't know a word, I had to look it up in my dictionary, and even that was hard. It was something that I could do at home, and I could do as much of it as I could stand.

I could stand a lot.

Getting on the Road Again

Fifteen months into my recovery, I had a couple of goals that I hadn't told anyone about, and they would have been a little far-fetched any earlier in the process. I wanted to travel on a real vacation again, and I wanted to drive a car (or at least try). Both would be key milestones to reclaiming my independence.

We had canceled a trip we had planned in 2009 because of my stroke, but now it was time to celebrate my progress with our long-delayed trip to Mexico for our five-year anniversary. We wanted a real vacation—no therapy and no doctors, just relaxing and having fun. However, the vacation was out of the country, which would be another first for me and us. By then, I had improved a lot. I could walk on my own with the WalkAide, although not fast. I could use my right arm but not perfectly. When we were out in public, though, I always had Brad right by my side. I felt good about where I was.

We stayed at a beautiful all-inclusive resort, in a great room, and we spent time by the pool and at the beach and ate in the resort restaurants. It was like getting a little piece of my old life back.

Even though we were in a different country, some things were the same. By the pool, in restaurants, and in other places, maybe without even realizing it, people pay special attention to anyone with disabilities. A woman wearing a bathing suit and a WalkAide was bound to get some stares. (Heck, sometimes I stared myself if I caught sight of my reflection or my shadow.) This resort didn't have any handrails to get into the pools, so whenever I got in, Brad would have to help me in, and I noticed people watching us with curiosity.

I tried to give them the benefit of the doubt. "They don't know they're making me uncomfortable," I said to Brad. "They don't mean anything by it."

Brad wasn't as forgiving.

"I guess maybe I was one of those people staring before my stroke," I replied. "I'm not sure I was always as kind and understanding as I should have been. It's so different now."

"It's probably like having a dog," Brad said, and I just looked at him. "No, wait—you know what I mean." He laughed. "I have no patience with dogs—or kids, for that matter—because I don't have one. But if you have a dog, you do have patience with all dogs."

I smiled and let him off the hook. "I know what you mean, babe. It's fine. It is what it is. I'm just happy to be here in this place with you, enjoying the sunshine."

The staff offered to escort us in a golf cart when we were going too far to walk, which made our stay even more comfortable.

I guess the lesson is that people can think what they want and stare all they want, but I could now check "international travel" off my list, and that was all I cared about.

Driving

Since my first day at the START facility in July 2010, I had spied a bigger challenge—the driving simulator—and thought to myself, *Hmm.*

I said to the OT person, "So that's a little driving simulator."

"Yes, but you're not ready yet."

"Could I ever even possibly do it?"

"Yes, I really think you might."

"Oh, really? Oh, that's very interesting."

We tabled that idea for the time being as I focused on more-achievable goals, but the simulator was there, in the middle of the room, almost always open. I watched with curiosity whenever there was a patient inside, trying to picture myself there.

Finally, after about four months of intensive therapy, my caseworker said, "Would you like to start the driving simulator? Are you even interested?"

"Of course I'm interested," I said, "but it makes me pretty nervous."

"There's nothing to be nervous about. We can try it. What's the worst that can happen?"

Good question. What was the worst thing that could happen? Maybe I wouldn't be able to do it, and then I just wouldn't be able to drive. I tried that thought on for size. *That would be okay,* I decided. I could live with that.

"Brad," I said one night at dinner, "what would you think if I could never drive again?"

"We're dealing with that now, and we can deal with that forever if that's the way it is." He was sensible and generous, as always.

To the simulator I went, where I crashed and burned over and over. I killed pedestrians and dogs and ran over stop signs. The problem was always in that right-side visual field cut. I realized I needed to do more exercises to improve that problem area, but I also realized I was afraid, and it was hard.

It took seemingly forever, but with every session, I got a little bit better. Once I really got it through my head that this was just a simulation and not reality, I was able to relax and just drive. It was actually kind of fun. Eventually, after about six months of practice (about twenty months into my recovery), the OT said, "Well, Kelly, I think you've got it. We have a partnership with a driving school that has adapted cars. Here's their number. I think you should call them."

You might think that I was all over that opportunity. Driving is the ultimate expression of independence, and wasn't that my goal? But I didn't call right away. I needed to think about this, and I thought for months.

What was stopping me? Well, I didn't want to fail. I had many other things going on, and I didn't want to take my focus off my other therapy. Furthermore, of course, there was the simple issue of safety. I was worried about my reaction time and my ability to actually handle a car on the road.

But I'd never know if I didn't try.

On the day of the first lesson, a female instructor drove the adaptive car to my house, and we spent half an hour in the driveway. I got familiar with the car, getting in and out, buckling and unbuckling the seat belt, and adjusting the mirrors. She showed me how the car had been adapted to allow me to operate the pedals with my left foot. I practiced using the spinner handle on the steering wheel. Then, whether I was ready or not, she drove us to a quiet spot on the street, not even a parking lot.

"All righty," she chirped. "Get in the driver's seat, and we'll just take it a little at a time and see how it goes."

I was like an old granny, driving slowly with my eyes darting from side to side on the lookout for cars, kids, and balls.

"It's okay," the instructor said. "I have a brake on my side. I'll keep you from hitting anything."

After what seemed like hours, I pulled to the side of the road, we switched places, and she drove us back to my driveway.

"Did I fail?" I asked her.

She laughed congenially. "No, no, no. You did great! We need to schedule another session, but that's a very good start."

We scheduled another session and then another. After about four sessions, the instructor was ready to be done with me, and she only had to slam on the brake once, when I gassed it instead of braking. She gave me the signed papers I would need to get my driver's license reinstated, and I was ready.

On the big day, Brad took me to the license bureau and waited with all the parents of sixteen-year-olds while I did my road test. I passed with flying colors. I was a driver again, if not the kind of driver I had once been. On the way home, Brad rode shotgun, scared to death but as proud as he could be.

I'm not ever going to be comfortable on the expressway again or with big trucks driving fast in the next lane. A couple of times a week, I drive to a few places that are familiar and easy. I only drive after 9:00 a.m. and before 4:00 p.m., when the roads are quiet. If I ever have a problem or experience anxiety about driving, then I just won't drive, and that is fine.

My new normal was really starting to take shape now, and nearly two years into my recovery, I had accomplished more than anyone had thought possible.

My New Birthday

We called the anniversary of my stroke my new birthday.

By the time the first one rolled around in August 2010, I felt positive that I was going to continue to improve. With the START program, I felt the sky was the limit, which was energizing for me.

By the time the second one rolled around, I felt like a new version of myself, Kelly 2.0. My normal personality was there but modified a little bit. I could even drive again.

As we rounded the corner of that second anniversary, we were told we'd made the 2012 calendar for the rehab facility. It was rewarding that of all the stories they could have told, they'd thought ours was one of the twelve best.

The best transition that happened during that year was that Brad was no longer my caregiver; we were a team. I felt much better about that. Brad would say, "Oh, I looked at something. Go online, and research some stuff while I'm working." I felt good that I wasn't just the invalid but could actually contribute, and I found that in some ways, I was even better at online research and more focused when organizing my thoughts.

Through this research, we discovered some surgical procedures that we thought might improve my quality of life.

Procedures to Adjust My Gait

I had been using the WalkAide for all of 2010 and into 2011 to help with dorsiflexion. The doctors also tried some medical interventions to address my gait. First, they tried Botox, but that never allowed me to get my heel down without the WalkAide. The next option was a phenol block, which goes right into the nerve and stops anything from getting past it. The idea was to interrupt the signals the brain was sending to the calf, so it couldn't fire and push my foot down.

The first phenol block in 2010 was a godsend, because I could immediately get my heel down, even in a gym shoe. Little by little, I weaned myself from the cumbersome WalkAide and began to feel even more like a normal person, just one with a little limp.

Some people only get one or two phenol blocks, and then their foot works normally again without the phenol, but for me, that was not to be. Although the phenol block worked to get my heel down, my toes started curling, crunching up in my shoes and causing significant pain. We consulted with the chief rehabilitation specialist in the START program for options.

"Well, you could consider surgery," he said. "The orthopedic guys could cut your tendons and loosen your Achilles tendon. That could give you some relief."

I think it's like any medical issue—the doctors try the least invasive solution first and then try the next option and the next one. Surgery is obviously a last resort, which we got to through the normal progression of different options.

I had never had any type of surgery before the stroke. I'd never had a broken bone or even stitches. But I wasn't afraid of needles, pain, surgery, or the fact that the first available date was, ironically, on Friday the Thirteenth. If there was a procedure that could help me regain or retain function, I was all in.

The old me would have hesitated, but Kelly 2.0 had a new level of clarity, and Brad was supportive despite his fear of me going under anesthesia for that long.

The first surgery was successful in September 2011, and I eventually had two more leg and foot procedures to improve my heel strike and gait. The second surgery was what is called a full bridle procedure, which involves a tibial tendon transfer and reattachment. It helped with my drop foot. I also eventually had my toe knuckles permanently pinned to stop the curling. Both these surgeries had six- to eight-week recovery times, and I was in a non-weight-bearing cast and boot during that time. This presented its own unforeseen issues since I couldn't use crutches, but we discovered that a combination of a walker and a knee scooter allowed me to get around safely. During that time, day-to-day activity was really hard. It was worth it in the end, but one of the hardest things I've done was getting around with a walker and one good arm for eight weeks and repeating similar procedures twice more in two years. While the surgeries were successful, I still require Botox in my arm and leg and have phenol blocks to help me walk. Importantly, we found all these advanced recovery options through our own research, yet again proof that you can continue to find ways to improve your life, but it's up to you.

The Journey Back to Me

I was still trying to figure out what I wanted to do in the future, but I realized during that second year that I couldn't just map out my life like I used to.

Just prior to the surgery in September, we decided we would commit to our first trip to Napa Valley that October. Once again, I set a goal to be able to travel with a walking boot within four weeks of surgery. I must have been crazy, but I had to make it, because it would be a combination celebration of my progress in two years, my foot surgery, and our sixth wedding anniversary. Brad made the plane reservations using his frequent flyer points, but the rest of the planning was on me. I researched lodging options, wineries, and restaurants. Getting back into planning mode made me feel like my old self again.

We hit all the usual Napa tourist attractions, including the train, several wineries, and a gondola ride, and we visited the Golden Gate Bridge on the way.

"Just think, Kelly," Brad said one night at dinner. "Two years ago, you were in a virtual coma in the hospital. One year ago, we went to Mexico, and you were wearing the WalkAide and needed so much help still."

"And look at me now!" I said. "We are together on a fantastic anniversary trip. I'm back!"

All the hard work, surgeries, and sacrifices had gotten us to that point. We had come to terms with our new normal for me and for us as a couple. I looked out at the sun setting behind the rolling hills covered with vineyards.

I was again excited about each day and what lay ahead for us together as a couple, and I smiled, held his hand, and thought to myself, *I'm back*.

If We Only Knew: Travel and Driving Strategy

- Be aware of the challenges that airports present. Even if you don't need a wheelchair on a daily basis, airports are different. You should indicate wheelchair assistance in your itinerary and research the terminals and gates. Don't be afraid to tell TSA you have a handicap. They will usually escort you through the line. If you walk, be aware of the crowds of people, as they will knock you over if you can't see them coming. Most airports have some type of executive shuttle. We recommend this instead of driving and parking, as the shuttle takes you right to the terminal and ends up costing about the same as daily parking.

- With international travel, customs can be challenging if your assistance doesn't show up and you don't know the language. You want as few luggage pieces as possible in case you have to carry them or get a cart.

- Carefully research hotels and resorts. As you plan your trip, scout the layout of the resort or hotel on the Internet. Make sure the shower in your room has grab bars or is a walk-in. Ask for a room by the elevator or the areas where you plan to spend the most time. In our case, we don't need or want completely handicap-accessible rooms with lower beds and shower curtains, because we don't have a wheelchair, but we do want to minimize the walking required to get where we want to go. Some resorts have golf carts. Look for railings in and around pools and beach access, and let the staff know before you arrive that you have some limitations. These little things will add up to a better trip, as your handicap will be less of a distraction.

- With regard to driving, you'll be happy to know that there are adaptations for cars for people with weakness on one side, especially the right side. I have an adaptive gas pedal and steering knob that help me drive with my good arm and leg. Most auto dealers have reimbursement programs for adding these types of adaptations, and you get to figure out which one is best for you during the driving school.

- Getting a driver's license is not out of the question. You might have to take the driving test again to get your license back, but the driving school will help you figure out what adaptations you need and help you feel safer and confident. Be prepared for your state to require proof that you are capable, including bringing a note from your neurologist, passing the test, and reconfirming every year that you are not a seizure risk. Ask for e-mail and online ways to keep the appropriate parties updated so that you don't have to wait on everything in the mail.

- Practice. I practiced a lot in a school parking lot even after my test to be comfortable, and I still don't drive on the highway, but I did for my test. I can get where I need to go, and that helps me be more independent. You can do it!

EPILOGUE

The Future

Kelly

The day that everything changed—that's how we still think of the day of the stroke. We were living a life that was amazing—perfect. We took it all for granted, which is just human nature, I guess, especially when you're young. Only after you endure a life-altering event do you realize how easily it can all be taken away from any of us in an instant.

Some of the doctors warned us about problems that can take hold in relationships after a health problem like this, especially when you don't know for sure what's going to happen. I always worried about Brad, because caregiving is a lot of work, a lot of balls to juggle. The doctors warned us that about 50 percent of couples divorce in the first six months when one of them has to care for the other. It's a big responsibility.

My stroke was the beginning of the most amazing relationship. I always thought our relationship was great. We were like peas in a pod, and I loved him. We always had fun, and we had a good life together. But now it's a whole new level of fun and honesty, and we love each other more, which is weird because I didn't think we could love each other more.

The deepening of our relationship didn't happen right away, and for a while, it didn't seem so good, but now we're stronger by far. We talked before, but we did not talk like we do now. We talked about nothing and funny things but not real things. The past five years have been a journey to something magical and real versus something just normal and routine. It's a crazy level that I don't know a lot of other people ever get to.

I think my stroke was more devastating to him in many ways than it was to me. Maybe it sounds terrible to say, but I've lived a full life. Even before the stroke, I felt I had pretty much done everything I wanted to do, and I often felt that if I couldn't survive, I would be okay with that. A lot of people say, "I want this and that," but I thought, *I've done so many wonderful things that I would be okay with not doing anything else.*

However, I knew that Brad wouldn't have been okay with that. I could see that he needed me in a way I hadn't seen before, and I had to fight every step of the way to get better for him.

I didn't want to be a burden or to have him to worry about me. But now I think he wanted to watch those sessions because he was proud. He's proud of me and the work we've done together, and I think he's proud of himself and the man he's become. He should be.

Before the stroke, Brad and I were so busy making our life and our careers that we never thought about anything else. We never talked about deep things. We thought everything was perfect that way, but when I look back now, I can see how much we were missing by sticking with this model of so-called perfection. I have come to like messy things a little bit. I like laughing about it, crying about it, and being honest.

Looking Ahead

Life is never all rosy and wonderful. In one moment, I'm happy-go-lucky, and then I drop a plate or can't open a jar, and I get frustrated. Everything takes much more time than I thought. I made much more progress in the first year than the second year, but I only got really better in the third and fourth years. That was when I felt saner. I think I didn't know that until I got there.

I'm still trying to get better every day. It's not a job with a paycheck, but it's full-time, and I have to do it. If I skip out on working out or doing exercises, then I could lose the progress I've made.

I know I'm different now. I accept that there are things I'm not going to be able to do, and I'm going to have to deal with it. For example, my thought process is still slower than it once was, and I still mix up my words, so I like to think about what I'm going to say before I respond—and not every conversation partner affords me that chance.

But I don't dwell on the few things the stroke has permanently changed for me that I can't do anything about; instead, I focus my attention on what I can do and can control. Last year, we built a new house, and I was the one meeting with the builders and keeping them on track. I was able to make decisions about design, decorating, and landscaping. Who would have thought, in the fall of 2009, that I would have come this far?

Since my stroke, I feel as if I am more real, more present. I realize that in spite of my meditation and my faith, I was never really present in my life, just in the now and not worried or thinking about other things. My life is richer; the ups and downs are more interesting. I'm more genuine now.

I have amazing faith, although I really hated God for a little bit. I had plenty of "Why me?" moments. However, eventually, I surrendered and said, "Okay, God. I get it. Just let me know what the next chapter is in my life."

I believe that God could see that I needed to rest and knew a stroke was what it would take to get my attention. We still don't know the cause of my stroke, but I just say, "Okay, God, I heard you."

I feel blessed that I survived, and I don't worry too much about why this happened to me. I think that right now, it's my time to focus on me and on my husband, and I believe it's important to help Brad with his job. I look toward the future now and think about the exciting things we do that maybe we would otherwise not have done until we were older. We do them now just in case.

I want to travel again, though I doubt we'll be spending twelve hours a day on foot sightseeing, as we used to. I can't ever run a marathon, as I'd hoped to. I can't run at all. I thought I was going to run; I said that in the first year, and it's now about to be the fifth year, and I don't know that it's ever going to happen. But I'm okay with that. I can walk, even if I have a limp. I don't know that I will ever be able to work again, but I hope I can find a way to help other people, maybe people who have had similar issues. I believe I have a lot still to give to the world.

Everybody has issues, and these are mine.

You Are More Resilient Than You Know

I firmly believe the best thing that could have ever happened to me was having a stroke. I believe that with all my heart, and I think about it all the time. I know now in a way I never did before that every day is a blessing; it's a gift.

What I hope people take away from my story is inspiration for overcoming obstacles and remaining optimistic in the face of huge challenges. Resilience is what I'm talking about. I've always been fortunate to be a glass-half-full kind of person, and that positive outlook surely helps now. I get frustrated, but I always try to go full circle, back to the blessings.

I don't know about God's plan for my future. Maybe he needed me to rest up for something else in the future. I don't know what's going to happen next, but I'm okay with that now. Before, I always wanted to know what was coming. I still want to plan things, and I like to know what our schedule is, such as what we're doing for dinner tonight and what's going on for the weekend. That's my thing.

But for the long-term future, I'm okay with not knowing. The truth is, we never know, and life can change in an instant. Make the most of today!

LESSONS LEARNED

The literature is correct in saying strokes don't happen only to an individual; they also happen to all those closest to that person. We cannot thank those involved in our journey enough, from the first responders at the airport to the weekend neurosurgery staff and emergency room team at St. Elizabeth Hospital, the University of Cincinnati's neurological ICU, HealthSouth, The Drake Center, and everyone involved in my continued rehabilitation.

We'd like to leave you with some of the lessons we learned along the way, condensed into the essential messages we believe will be helpful to others facing stroke or other traumatic brain injuries.

It's up to you, but you're not alone.

Brad Patients with brain injuries do have some degree of control over how far their recovery can take them. You get out what you put in.

Kelly We were never the kind of people who thought therapy would help us, but those sessions enabled us, mostly me, to work through the new emotions I was feeling and put it all out there.

Believe in possibilities.

Brad If someone had told Kelly in those first therapy sessions how long it would take her to get her vocabulary and cognitive function back, she would have probably been depressed.

Kelly As I think about it now, it seems likely that none of the medical professionals, or maybe even my family, believed it was possible for me to get back to my old self 100 percent, but not a single person said that to me. It was important for me to believe in that possibility, especially in the beginning.

Stand up for yourself.

Brad You need a quarterback. As the caregiver to a severely ill or injured loved one, you are his or her voice and advocate. The survivor needs you more than ever.

Kelly I learned from this experience that there are situations in life in which you have to put yourself first. No matter how much you love to serve others and support your family, sometimes you have to be selfish.

Communication takes work.

Brad During that period when I saw Kelly unable to match simple cards or remember basic words, I was terrified. What I know now is that abilities can come back a lot faster than when you learned them the first time.

Kelly My communication skills are different from the way they were before. I am not as articulate, and sometimes I have to search for the right word or will say the wrong word. That's okay. I worry less about offending people and am more straightforward and direct than I used to be.

It's not over when you go home.

Brad As desperate as we were to get Kelly home from rehab, I knew being at home would be harder. Prepare, and be patient.

Kelly The doctors told me napping was important, but I had no idea. It's the most important aspect of recovery, and I still carve out time to rest each day.

You will face lots of unknowns and unpredictability.

Brad We all want to think that medicine is an exact science and that the doctors have all the answers. What I know now is that when it comes to the brain, it's not, and they don't.

Kelly I have learned to embrace my new normal, and so has Brad. We are both enormously proud of what we have accomplished together.

WEBSITE RESOURCE LIST

National Associations—Signs, Symptoms, and Support

- American Heart Association
  http://www.strokeassociation.org/STROKEORG/
- National Stroke Association
  http://www.stroke.org/site/PageNavigator/HOME
- Centers for Disease Control and Prevention
  http://www.cdc.gov/stroke/signs_symptoms.htm

Hospitals and Rehab

- http://health.usnews.com/best-hospitals/rankings/neurology-and-neurosurgery
- http://www.womenschoiceaward.com/awarded/best-hospitals/stroke-care/
- https://www.stroke.org/sites/default/files/resources/NSAFactSheet_ChoosingaStrokeRehabProvider_2014.pdf
- http://uchealth.com/services/long-term-acute-care/stroke-recovery/

Home Adaptation and Tools

- http://www.strokecenter.org/patients/caregiver-and-patient-resources/home-modification/adapting-the-home-after-a-stroke/
- http://www.especialneeds.com/
- http://www.rehabmart.com/

- http://www.stroke4carers.org/?tag=adaptations
- http://www.stroke-rehab.com/adaptive-equipment.html

Stroke Networks—Information, Education, and Community

- http://www.strokenetwork.org/
- http://youngstroke.org/
- http://www.healthfulchat.org/stroke-chat-room.html
- https://www.facebook.com/Greater-Cincinnati-Stroke-Consortium

Traumatic Brian Injury—Information and Education

- http://www.traumaticbraininjury.com/

Kentucky Traumatic Brian Injury (TBI) Trust Fund—Funding Resource for TBI Survivors in Kentucky

- http://chfs.ky.gov/dail/braintrust.htm
- http://mchb.hrsa.gov/programs/traumaticbraininjury/statefact sheets.html
- http://www.acl.gov/Programs/AoD/TBI/Index.aspx

Guardianship

- http://waiting.com/guardianship.html
- http://www.traumaticbraininjury.com/funding-resources/guardian ship/
- http://braininjuryeducation.org/Topics/Guardianship/

READING LIST

Bolte Taylor, Jill. *My Stroke of Insight*. New York: Viking, 2008.

Fisher, Andrew. *Surviving a Stroke*. Louisville: Butler Books, 2011.

Hutton, Cleo. *After a Stroke: 300 Tips for Making Life Easier.* New York: Demos Health, 2005.

McEwen, Mark. *Change in the Weather: Life after Stroke*. New York: Gotham, 2008.

Brett, Doris. *The Twelfth Raven: A Memoir of Stroke, Love, and Recovery.* Western Australia: UWA, 2014.

Twomey, Maureen. *Before, Afdre, and After.* California: published by author, 2015.

Levine, Peter. *Stronger after Stroke: Your Roadmap to Recovery*. New York: Demos Health, 2012.

Waters, Marlys J. *Stroke Victims Have Rights: All about Strokes and Recovery.* California: CreateSpace, 2016.

Guns, Bob. *Rewire Your Brain, Rewire Your Life: A Handbook for Stroke Survivors and Their Caregivers*. Livermore, CA: Wingspan Press, 2008.

Genova, Lisa. *Left Neglected*. New York: Gallery Books, 2011.

APPENDIX A

START Program Assessment Report

REHABILITATION SCREEN

System	Sign or Symptom	No	Yes (explain the problem)
1. Communication	Difficulty speaking, finding words or being understood, mumbling, slurring	NO	
2. Swallowing	Difficulty eating, drinking, or chewing, choking, coughing or gagging, drooling, feeling as if food is caught in mouth or throat	NO	
3. Voice	Change in loudness or tone of voice, hoarseness	NO	
4. Ears	Difficulty hearing	NO	
5. Thinking Skills (Cognition)	Difficulty with memory, attention, planning, problem solving, and organizing your thoughts.	NO	
6. Activities of Daily Living	Difficulty with bathing, grooming, feeding, toileting, uses adaptive equipment to complete tasks	NO	
7. Home Management	Difficulty with cooking, cleaning, bills, living independently	NO	[illegible] Dinner
8. Hand Splint	Do you currently wear a hand splint on your affected arm?	NO	
9. Exercise/ Workout	Difficulty doing an exercise program for your arm and/or leg?	NO	
10. Transfers	Difficulty with standing up, getting into bed, getting on/off the toilet, getting in/out of the car	N	
11. Balance	Have you fallen in the past year?		yes - January 2010
12. Walking	Difficulty walking by yourself?	NO	Does someone provide assistance? Do you use a cane/walker? How far can you go?
13. Orthotic/Brace	Do you currently wear a leg brace on your affected leg?	NO	yes - Walkaid
14. Wheelchair	Do you currently rely on a wheelchair for mobility in the house and community?	NO	How old is your wheelchair?
15. Recreation/ Quality of Life	Do have concerns about how your stroke has affected you socially with leisure activities? Hobbies?	NO	

Nine Symptom Checklist

Patient Name Kelly Marsh DOB 3-5-73

Appointment Date June 22, 2010

Over the last 2 weeks, how often have you been bothered by any of the following problems?

1. Little interest or pleasure in doing things
✓ not at all (0) ___ several days (1) ___ more than half the days (2) ___ nearly every day (3)

2. Feeling down, depressed or hopeless
✓ not at all (0) ___ several days (1) ___ more than half the days (2) ___ nearly every day (3)

3. Trouble falling or staying asleep or sleeping too much
✓ not at all (0) ✓ several days (1) ___ more than half the days (2) ___ nearly every day (3)

4. Feeling tired or having little energy
✓ not at all (0) ___ several days (1) ___ more than half the days (2) ___ nearly every day (3)

5. Poor appetite or overeating
___ not at all (0) ___ several days (1) ✓ more than half the days (2) ___ nearly every day (3)

6. Feeling bad about yourself or feeling that you are a failure or have left yourself or your family down
___ not at all (0) ✓ several days (1) ___ more than half the days (2) ___ nearly every day (3)

7. Trouble concentrating on things such as reading the newspaper or watching television
___ not at all (0) ___ several days (1) ✓ more than half the days (2) ___ nearly every day (3)

8. Moving or speaking so slowly that other people could have noticed or the opposite – being so fidgety or restless that you have been moving around a lot more than usual
___ not at all (0) ✓ several days (1) ___ more than half the days (2) ___ nearly every day (3)

9. Thoughts that you would be better off dead or hurting yourself in some way
✓ not at all (0) ___ several days (1) ___ more than half the days (2) ___ nearly every day (3)

TOTAL SCORE: 6

If you have checked off ANY problems, how difficult have these problems made it for you to do your work, take care of things at home or get along with other people?

___ Not difficult at all ✓ Somewhat difficult ___ Very difficult ___ Extremely difficult

BAKAS CAREGIVING OUTCOMES SCALE

Patient Name *Kelly Marsh* DOB *3/5/73*

Caregiver's Name *Brad Marsh* Appointment Date *6/22/10*

This group of questions is about the possible changes in your life from providing care for the stroke survivor. For each possible change listed, circle one number indicating the degree of change. The numbers indicating the degree of change range from -3 "Changed for the Worst" to +3 "Changed for the Best". The number 0 indicates "Did Not Change".

AS RESULT OF PROVIDING CARE FOR THE STROKE SURVIVOR:	Changed for the Worst			No Change	Changed for the Best		
1. My self esteem	-3	-2	-1	0	+1	**(+2)**	+3
2. My physical health	-3	-2	-1	0	+1	**(+2)**	+3
3. My time for family activities	-3	-2	-1	0	+1	**(+2)**	+3
4. My ability to cope with stress	-3	-2	-1	0	**(+1)**	+2	+3
5. My relationship w/ friends	-3	-2	-1	0	+1	**(+2)**	+3
6. My future outlook	-3	-2	-1	0	+1	**(+2)**	+3
7. My level of energy	-3	-2	-1	0	+1	**(+2)**	+3
8. My emotional well being	-3	-2	-1	0	**(+1)**	**(+2)**	+3
9. My roles in life	-3	-2	-1	0	**(+1)**	+2	+3
10. My time for social activities with friends	-3	-2	-1	0	+1	**(+2)**	+3
11. My relationship with family	-3	-2	-1	0	+1	**(+2)**	+3
12. My financial well being	-3	-2	-1	0	**(+1)**	+2	+3
13. My relationship with the stroke survivor	-3	-2	-1	0	**(+1)**	+2	+3
14. My physical functioning	-3	-2	-1	0	**(+1)**	+2	+3
15. My general health	-3	-2	-1	0	+1	**(+2)**	+3
16. In general, how has your life changed as a result of taking care of the stroke survivor	-3	-2	-1	0	+1	**(+2)**	+3

IF THERE ARE ANY OTHER CHANGES IN YOUR LIFE AS A RESULT OF PROVIDING CARE FOR THE STROKE SURVIVOR, PLEASE WRITE THE BELOW & RATE THEM ACCORDINGLY.

	Changed for the Worst			No Change	Changed for the Best		
17.	-3	-2	-1	0	+1	+2	+3
18.	-3	-2	-1	0	+1	+2	+3
19.	-3	-2	-1	0	+1	+2	+3

Dear **Ms. Marsh:**

Thank you for coming to the Stroke Recovery Center at Drake Center on **6/22/09**. Our multidisciplinary team comprehensively evaluates stroke recovery across multiple domains such as motor deficits and cognitive changes. Based on our assessments and our discussion with you, the following domains in your stroke recovery were identified:

ASSESSMENT

1) Motor Deficits- **You have some residual right sided weakness from your stroke. You have difficulty with walking due to weakness in your ankle and some spasticity in your right leg. Balance testing suggested that you are at a low risk for falls.**
2) Sensory Deficits- **You have a subjective 25-50% sensory deficit throughout your right side as a result of stroke.**
3) Speech- **You have difficulty with expressive language function, including word finding problems and occasional errors/substitutions. Your receptive function appears normal. You are relatively well compensated due to your high pre-stroke ability.**
4) Cognitive- **Cognitive testing showed a score of 23/30 (with 26/30 being normal). You struggled with complex tasks. You have recently seen a neuropsychologist at HealthSouth.**
5) Vision- **A right inferior visual field cut was noted.**
6) Emotional/Psychological- **The PHQ-9 score was 7. This suggests that you do not have active depression and/or anxiety at this time. You are currently taking Celexa. You may have had some anxiety issues and some obsessive/compulsive behaviors that have been less noticeable since the stroke.**
7) Symptomatic management- **You have spasticity in your right upper extremity, and had botox for your right lower extremity 1 month ago. You have seizures that are successfully managed with Keppra. You take Trazadone for sleep.**
8) Caregiver support/stroke education- **Your husband is an excellent provider. You are a good team who are very knowledgeable about stroke and aggressive in seeking care for recovery. Your husband is at some risk for caregiver burnout due to stress at work while he is simultaneously worrying about you. There seems to be some stress between your family and your husband.**
9) Medications and Stroke prevention- **You are not currently taking any medications for stroke prevention at this time.**
10) Wellness- **You have a reasonably high level of physical activity and you are working hard to improve your neurologic function.**

GOALS:

Based on our assessments and our discussions with you, we are establishing the following goals:

1.) Improve language function.
2.) Improve leg/walking function.
3.) Improve fine motor control in right upper extremity.
4.) Return to driving.

Based upon our assessment, in combination with your goals for stroke recovery, we recommend the following:

PLAN

1) Physical Therapy: **Refer for further therapy to improve function and endurance, and to enhance your exercise and stretching program. We will expand your current training program to include more balance activities and use of Walk Aide which has worked to break you out of the stiff knee pattern. Can continue to use cyclic functional e-stim. May include work in the pool as well.**
2) Occupational Therapy: **Refer for further therapy to improve upper extremity function and endurance, and to enhance your exercise and stretching program. Repeat driver testing. Will include forced use/constraint induced therapy. We will provide a resting splint. Will try sensory re-education.**
3) Speech/Language Pathology: **Referral for further therapy to improve high-level language function including outside activities; consider working with InReturn or other vocational type activities in short term.**
4) Cognitive: **We will continue to evaluate your cognitive function while in therapy. We would like to obtain any neuropsychometric testing results that you have already completed.**
5) Emotional/Psychological: **There is no evidence of depression and/or anxiety at this time. Continue to take Celexa at the present dose and we will continue to monitor for symptoms. You are planning to start psychotherapy both as a couple and individually based upon your previous evaluation at HealthSouth.**
6) Research: **You are a candidate for the L300 study but you are not interested because of the control group in the study that only recieves an AFO and you do not want to wear an AFO. You also are a candidate for our upper extremity mental practice study, will start this while beginning driver evaluation (i.e. before formal OT described above). You may also consider an aphasia study with Dr. Szaflarski, such as constraint induced language therapy.**
7) Symptomatic management: **You should continue to receive botox as needed for spasticity. Continue Keppra for seizures. Consider discontinuing trazadone?**
8) Caregiver: **Your husband should keep up the good work as your advocate, and continue to help you as needed although you are largely independent. Watch for signs of caregiver stress and burnout. Proceed with psychotherapy as mentioned above.**
9) Medications and Stroke Prevention: **Continue current regimen without change, except to add an enteric coated aspirin daily for stroke and cardiac event prevention. You should follow up with PCP to follow for risk factor monitoring.**
10) Wellness: **Continue to stay active and increase activity as tolerated. Consider taking on some new challenges, including short term vocational work (InReturn) or the challenge of starting and maintaining a young stroke support group.**

We will review your progress in **12-16 weeks**. Thereafter, we will determine when you should return to clinic. If you have any questions, please do not hesitate to contact us by phone or email.

Sincerely,

The Stroke Recovery Team at Drake.

APPENDIX B

Medical File Checklist

How people organize the information varies. Some people use paper binders and folders, and others use spreadsheets or electronic programs, such as Microsoft Health Vault (https://www.healthvault.com/us/en), CareSync (http://caresync.com/consumers/index.php), HealthIT.gov (https://www.healthit.gov/patients-families/maintain-your-medical-record), WebMD (http://www.webmd.com/phr), or one of many others. The information in the file will change as treatment progresses, but the elements below were the most helpful elements in our health file.

Insurance and Billing

- Consider keeping a copy of your insurance card in the front of the file, where you can easily access it. That way, you'll have the name, ID number, and contact number readily available. If the print on the card is small, you might want to enlarge the copy of the card or just write the information on the folder so that you can easily read it when you need to without having to find the card and squint at the print through tired eyes.

- Make sure you have the names, titles, direct-line phone numbers, and e-mail addresses for insurance company contacts. Keep a separate log for phone calls, and include the date, the time of the call, whom you spoke with, and the outcome of the call or the answer to your question.

- Make sure you have the name, title, direct-line phone number, and e-mail address for anyone in hospital billing. You should also log billing-related phone calls with the date, time, person you spoke with, and outcome of the call or answer to your question.

- Keep copies of any explanations of benefits and bills if you're given paper copies.

- Write down any procedures you might need to monitor. For example, we had to have a certain procedure in place for the insurance company to cover therapy at home, and we had to call to ensure progress reports were filed so that the sessions were covered. Know what your procedures are, and create a checklist to make following up easier.

Hospital Staff

- Make sure you have the names, titles, direct-line phone numbers, and e-mail addresses for social workers.

- Document the names of all the doctors and their specialties, as well as next steps they tell you are in the plan for observation and treatment. Ask if they are affiliated with a private group in addition to the hospital. Most are, and that is how scheduling happens and how you can get messages to them in addition to the nursing staff. Get as much contact information as you can for the doctor.

- Make sure you have your therapists' names, titles, phone numbers, e-mail addresses, and affiliations.

- Record the names of nurses and nurse's aides and their shifts so that you can share them with other family members. You might also be able to get the phone numbers or e-mail addresses for the nurses.

Patient Information and Schedule

- List any dietary restrictions or allergies. Keep this on a separate page with your contact information at the top, and make copies so that you can give one out in writing to anyone and everyone who seems to need it.

- Keep a list of medicines and what each is supposed to do. You might have to update this list frequently. Keep it on a separate page so that you can give it to anyone who needs to have it.

- Keep track of testing and treatment that's happening (MRIs, CT, blood work, angiograms, craniotomies, cranioplasties, PEG tubes, AVM, ventilators, etc.). Keep copies of the results if you can, in case you need to change doctors and give the information to another doctor quickly.

- Keep track of any changes to the treatment plan.

- Note visiting hours and the daily schedules for medicine, personal needs, and doctors' check-in times—you don't want to show up and miss the doctor, who might be in surgery and unavailable.

Made in United States
Orlando, FL
21 June 2022